Life on a Road Less Traveled

Or, Memoirs from Behind the Scenes of History

LOUDELL INSLEY

BOOKSIDE Press

Copyright © 2022 by Loudell Insley

ISBN: 978-1-998784-41-7 (Paperback)
978-1-998784-42-4 (Hardback)
978-1-998784-43-1 (E-book)

All rights reserved. No part of this publication may be reproduced, distributed, or transmitted in any form or by any means, including photocopying, recording, or other electronic or mechanical methods, without the prior written permission of the publisher, except in the case brief quotations embodied in critical reviews and other noncommercial uses permitted by copyright law.

The views expressed in this book are solely those of the author and do not necessarily reflect the views of the publisher, and the publisher hereby disclaims any responsibility for them. Some names and identifying details in this book have been changed to protect the privacy of individuals.

BookSide Press
877-741-8091
www.booksidepress.com
orders@booksidepress.com

CONTENTS

Preface vi
Introduction vii
Chapter One: Not Quite the Peace Corps 1
Chapter Two: How on Earth Did You Get That Job? 13
Chapter Three: Inside a Presidential Campaign 33
Chapter Four: Overcoming Tragedies 78
Chapter Five: Beyond Capitol Hill—A Different World 114
Chapter Six: Mess with Democracy, Go to Jail 126
Chapter Seven: Frank Perdue—Tough Man, Tender Chickens 149
Chapter Eight: Real Estate Is Definitely Not Boring 170
Chapter Nine: Outward Bound—Have I Lost My Mind? 184
Chapter Ten: Boca Raton: A Rarified World 208
Chapter Eleven: A Spiritual Journey 227
Chapter Twelve: Who Says You Can't Go Home Again? 237
Epilogue 250
Acknowledgments 253

With love and appreciation to my parents, my brother, and my brother's family. Thank you for being my safety net and my encouragers. But mostly, thank you for surrounding me with love.

PREFACE

Looking back on your life and visualizing the paths you took and the ones you skipped, do you wonder what your life would have been like if you had taken the other path? I have. Some you regret taking and wish there could be a second chance; others had good results and perhaps you wondered how you could have been so wise to have chosen that path at that time and had such a good outcome. In the end, for the most part, my choices surprised me. The results pleased me.

Have you ever felt the hand of God guiding you? I have. There have been many times I've felt his hand on my shoulder, turning me this way or that, although sometimes it's been a swift kick in the butt. Whatever… it worked. The result has been a wonderful life. Here are some of my memories.

INTRODUCTION

When I tell people I am writing a book, their first question is usually "What's your book about?"

My answer is "Me."

When that bit of information draws a blank stare, I explain that over the years of my childhood, as we sat around the dinner table, my brother, Phil, and I asked Mother and Dad questions about their lives. How did you meet? What was it like in the "olden days"? What was it like to do… whatever? They would entertain us with their stories.

Since I have no children asking for my stories, and since I have lived in a nestbed of Republicans who have little interest in them anyway, and since I inherited Dad's penchant for telling those very stories, I have decided to write them down so my family will have them, even if they don't want to hear them!

I did not keep a diary as I went along, so I am telling these stories as I remember them. If there are factual errors, they are all mine. I can tell you now that some of the names have been changed—not necessarily to protect the guilty, but simply because I can't remember them.

A friend recently told me that when we were in high school he thought I was a princess. I laughed and told him I had thought he was the golden boy. We were both surprised by the other's perception, for neither of us recognized ourselves when viewed through the other's eyes. Even so, if princesses are loved and protected, then I guess I was one. Even so, princesses have restrictions and parental expectations. And I was no exception. Those parental expectations included marriage and children. And they were mine too. Except I wanted to "live a little" before beginning my happy little family.

Love can be like a golden cage: it's pretty but confining. It seemed to me that my high school and college years were spent dreaming of escaping the cage and finally being my own person. That I have been able to do so is a testimony to my parents' love and patience, for they gave me the room to try my wings, to soar to surprising heights, and to crash into depths of despair. Without knowing they had my back, I'm not certain I would have taken some of the paths I did.

So, to my parents, a warm, heartfelt thank-you for being you and for being my financial and emotional safety net, which allowed me the luxury to take some unusual paths that ultimately enriched my life.

My brother, Phil, and his wife, Jacquie, have been so important in so many ways in my life that I want to also thank them for being my strength when I needed it and my coconspirators in most things.

After all, I can still hear Mother admonishing Phil, even as a youngster, to look after his younger sister while they were out for the evening. Even then I felt a twinge of sympathy for him because it was a rather large burden for such a young boy. But he took it on as well as he could, which is why my early childhood memories are of sore arms—Phil tried to get me to obey him by giving me Indian burns. (For those who missed out on that childhood torture, which we all did to each other, one grabs the victim's arm with both hands and twists his hands in opposite directions, leaving a "burn" mark on the arm. It's designed to hurt, and it does.)

And he continued looking out for me through the years, even coughing up the fake ID after I pleaded my case at dinner for the need of one. Mother looked up in bewilderment and asked, "Where would you get one?" I pointed to Phil. He went to his third-floor hideaway and reluctantly dipped into his stash of blank birth certificates to share with his sister. Then, as a family, we sat at the dinner table and filled out my fake ID while I swore liquor would never cross my lips until I was twenty-one.

He gave me a wonderful sister when he married Jacquie. She became my partner-in-crime as she served as my treasurer when I ran unsuccessfully for delegate to the 1976 Democratic convention. She encouraged my training as I prepared for Outward Bound. We answered for each other when people confused us for the other.

However, when I moved to the dark side to work for both Ted and Robert Kennedy, it put a crimp in our sibling conversations. The conservative physician and the liberal black sheep finally agreed to disagree and never, ever mention politics during an election year!

Eventually, my sister-in-law and I worked together on Phil's fortieth birthday party—the infamous Fish House Punch Party. For those who are not familiar with the punch from the Punch, let me say simply, it's almost pure rum, ramped up with some brandy and cognac and then cut only slightly with some sugar water and lemon juice. Turns out this was George Washington's favorite punch. No wonder.

On a hot June evening the cool, smooth punch, and hence the party, was a wild success, "wild" being the operative word. It took only a cup and a half to set nearly everyone on his ear. At some point, my date for the evening declared I most definitely needed a cup of coffee. Ordering me to remain in the den, he headed to the kitchen to get it. Never one to be dictated to, I followed along behind him. There we found the birthday boy, my surgeon brother, wiping up the floor by skating around with dish towels under each foot. In response to the news his sister needed coffee, he loyally reassured my horrified date, "Don't worry, we look after our own in this family," and then glided off on his towels.

Family—you gotta love 'em. They are the ones who keep you grounded. And they are the ones who pick you up and shove you back into the game, even when they think you're nuts. Such as before the Watergate scandal, when I had insisted something wasn't right in Washington. Something underhanded was going on, I just couldn't figure out what it was.

Loudell

CHAPTER ONE

NOT QUITE THE PEACE CORPS

Twenty years from now you will be more disappointed by the things you didn't do than by the ones you did do. So throw off the bowlines, sail away from the safe harbor. Catch the trade winds in your sails. Explore. Dream. Discover.
—Mark Twain

In 1962, between my junior and senior years in college, Mother had planned the ultimate European trip for me—first-class, nothing but the best: tea with the queen of England, a tour of the House of Dior, and sunbathing on the Riviera. It was to be a small tour of eight to ten young ladies who I am sure came from the best of families. Too bad the tour leader was diagnosed with cancer and had to cancel. It would have been a lovely trip.

Now Mother was stuck with nothing for me to do for the summer. You are probably wondering why I wasn't planning to work. As I look back on it, I wonder the same thing. In any case, that doesn't seem to have been a consideration.

Mother came up with Plan B: digging outhouses in the Andes. I got whiplash from the 180-degree switch from luxury to roughing it—with Methodist missionaries, no less.

When she made up her mind about something, she was a force to be reckoned with, and as I recall, my feeble complaints were futile from the start. She had the suitcases packed and I was on my way before I really comprehended what was up. Lucky for her I had always wanted to go to South America. Lucky for me she had heard me muttering that at some point.

I thought it was to be an interdenominational group of junior and senior college students from across the country on a work, travel, and study seminar. We would see Peru, Bolivia, Chile, and Argentina. I didn't read the fine print, since I had my marching orders from Mother. She was apparently comfortable with the fact there would be chaperones to look after her daughter. I was pretty much oblivious.

My instructions were to fly to the Miami airport and loiter near the Eastern Airlines ticket counter, where someone would pick me up. That being a much more trusting time than we have today, I did as I was told. Since I'd been instructed to bring my Bible, I was pretty confident I'd be able to pick out the leader of this group by her black outfit with starched white collar and ruffles at the wrist, and her Bible tucked securely under her arm. She'd probably hold her hands up in benediction and say, "Bless you, my child." I was pretty confident I had this whole scene pegged.

As I was sitting near the ticket counter waiting for someone to pick me up, I wondered if I should have my Bible under my arm as a signal. But since it was buried deep in my suitcase, I just sat there and wondered. Lo and behold, a man sporting casual clothes (and no Bible) walked right up to me, asked if I was Loudell, and said, "Welcome to the group. Come with me." So I did.

We went straight to a hotel room at the airport.

Our group consisted of twelve college students and two couples, who served as our chaperones. We passed the time relaxing in the room. It wasn't long before we had formed a big "friendship circle" and the leaders were asking us to introduce ourselves, tell what office we held in the Wesley Foundation (a campus organization of Methodist college students), and explain why we were on this trip and what we hoped to get out of it. So much for the ecumenicalism—no other denominations were represented.

I knew what Mother wanted out of it. She wanted me out of her hair for the summer while she worked on my brother Phil's wedding. It was news to me that I should have any reason for being with the group other than sightseeing, so I listened intently to what everyone else said.

The first person was treasurer of her Wesley Foundation, and she wanted to experience mission work. She hoped to become a missionary.

The second person was president of his local Wesley Foundation and had struggled to raise the money to finance this trip. He'd found different sponsors who chipped in, and he, too, wanted to learn more about the mission work.

The third person was regional vice president of the Wesley Foundation, and she was fascinated by the church and its mission work. The Rotary Club was sponsoring her, and on her return, she was to report back to them and give a speech about the trip.

And so it went until it got to me. I introduced myself and said I thought I had joined the Wesley Foundation since I seemed to be signing everything in sight during class registration and I recalled there was a card table for the Wesley Foundation near the exit. I think I signed something at their table. I explained that Plan A for the summer had fallen through and this was Plan B. And that I had no clue as to what I should expect to get out of this, other than completing my assigned task of buying ten silver cigarette boxes for my brother to give to the groomsmen at his wedding, and I certainly knew what I'd get when I got back if I didn't have the boxes!

That seemed to relieve those who followed me in the circle, and things became more relaxed. Eventually, we caught our plane and flew to Lima, Peru.

Well, when touring with a bunch of missionaries, one tends to see poverty, and that's what we saw. It was awful, it was depressing, and it wasn't long before I began to think about a good, stiff drink. Too bad I'd signed the pledge—no drinking while traveling with the Methodist (we don't drink) Church. This was going to be a very long trip.

So much for Peru. Off we went to Bolivia. By plane. At some point in my young adult life, I had vaguely thought what fun it would be to be a stewardess. Lucky her, getting to fly all over the world. It was on this trip to Bolivia that I scratched that tiny little thought off my list with a big, black mark.

In those days we were still flying in propeller-driven planes, and I think the planes flying into and out of Bolivia were of this type. In any case our group, fortified with a nice big, greasy breakfast, trooped onto the plane and flew up, up, up to Bolivia. Do you know that La Paz is the highest national capital in the world? And do you know that the airport, with its grass runway, is even higher? Neither did I.

As we approached the airport for our landing, the stewardess advised us to walk slowly when deplaning due to the lack of oxygen at high altitudes. Only last week a bull that had been shipped to La Paz from the United States for purposes of inseminating the Bolivian cows had broken free from his handlers and runoff, only to keel over and die of hypoxia right there in the airport. She had my attention. I'd crawl off if that would keep me alive.

As we came in for a landing, the pilot decompressed the airplane. Ears popped, stomachs gurgled, and people gagged. Then he touched down on that bumpy turf runway and bounced, bounced, bounced to a stop. And for four of our passengers, that heavy, greasy breakfast came up. (The little white bags that were to be used for this purpose really weren't large enough.) One person fainted. And all of us crawled out of the plane, albeit on our feet and not our hands and knees.

We were much the worse for wear. But golly gee, the first Peace Corps volunteers from the United States had also just arrived. Whether they were on our plane or not, I have no clue. But we were Americans, so we were rounded up and put into the official photo of the first Peace Corps volunteers.

We stayed in La Paz a night and a day to learn, once again, how to breathe. The natives were walking along the hilly cobblestone streets, showing off by carrying trunks and large pieces of furniture strapped to their backs. Being a poor country, there were few trucks available to carry things. The llamas certainly weren't going to carry heavy burdens, so the men did. They were awesome.

We were warned against doing two things: (1) taking photographs of the local people since they believed that cameras captured a piece of one's soul and kept it forever, and (2) chewing or drinking the cocoa leaves that were so popular among the local population!

They divided us into two groups. On the second day, my group was herded onto a cattle truck, complete with slated sides, and off we went to Ancarimes, a small village on the shores of Lake Titicaca. Located on an elevation above the airport, it is the highest salt lake in the world. We pitched and bounced and groaned our way there for about four hours.

We took a short potty break along the way. The men went to the right side of the road and the women to the left. There was a nice wall on our side so we all trooped behind the wall, squatted and did our thing, fishing around for Kleenex to finish it off. Our notion of having some privacy evaporated when we turned around to find the occupants of the house directly behind the wall sitting at their front door watching us tinkle in their yard.

Since we were below the equator, the season was late fall; and since we were high in the mountains, there were very few trees. This was, therefore, very desolate land. While there were mountains still reaching way above us, there was little color, just grayness. Perhaps at other times of the year things were more colorful. The poverty of the area was obvious, adding to the sense of desolation.

Finally, we arrived at our destination, which was a very small town with one street and a scattering of one-story adobe houses. On the outskirts of town, the missionaries had a two-story adobe building in which two female nurses lived on the lower floor and the education missionaries, a married couple, lived above. We four girls slept in sleeping bags on the downstairs floor, while the guys and our chaperones stayed with the married couple upstairs. There was one bathroom on each level; the toilets didn't work.

Looking just like something in an Andrew Wyeth painting, a rustic windmill slowly turned in the yard. It was able to generate just enough flow to collect water in the bathtub and to allow a slow trickle from the sink's faucet. There was a bucket sitting on the floor beside the toilet that we filled with water from the tub; we could then throw the water down the toilet bowl with enough velocity to actually cause it to flush. As each person emerged from the bathroom, we'd always check to see how proficient she was at this chore by asking how many buckets it took to flush the toilet. Nothing was sacred there. Eventually we were all able to do it with one bucket, but it took practice.

The missionaries cooked in big old iron stoves where wood is put into the innards and the fire from the burning wood did the baking and the stovetop cooking (just like at Appleby, my grandfather's home in Cambridge). They had no refrigeration, so we left the butter on the window sill, boiled all the water, and ate fresh food.

Our task was to build outhouses… one holers.

Each day we drove somewhere and dug a hole. The first location was a school—well, barely a school. No one had bathroom facilities. Squatters' rights literally was the rule. The local men brought us homemade adobe blocks that were strapped to the backs of their donkeys. We had a precast concrete slab with a hole in it that we placed over our pit, and then we built the walls around it. The villagers were to construct a thatched roof. And the missionaries were to teach the children what it was used for.

While we were working, the villagers fed us. We sat on the ground picnic-style. First there was soup made from slices of potato swimming in a thin, lightly seasoned water base. It was warm. Next came a platter of something like rice covered with what looked like an egg. That was okay. But sitting next to the egg were two kinds of potatoes, one round and one tubular (like a sweet potato). And that was the problem.

You see, the Indians grew potatoes for their cash crop. They sold the largest ones, ate the middle-sized ones, and kept the smallest ones for their seed crop. As a result, the potatoes they grew were getting smaller and smaller. The method used to preserve them for the year caused these small potatoes to wither and blacken until they looked just like what we were building the outhouses for. Those little turds were sitting on our dinner plates. And we were supposed to eat them!

When our native guides/translators realized we were avoiding these delicacies, they directed our attention to the villagers sitting huddled on the ground a little distance away, watching us eat. He pointed out that they were not eating because they'd given us their lunch. Obviously, we could not not eat those little turds. God knows we tried, but in the end, we sat and watched as our guide ate them for us.

As a result of the effects of the high altitude, strenuous physical labor, and our poor eating habits, we were always ravenously hungry. We were eating the nurses out of house and home. When they returned from an emergency trek to La Paz for provisions, we girls sat like a pack of wolves hungrily watching them unpack gunny sacks full of loaves of delicious bread, which they then whacked with their hands to knock off the extra flour. There was so much flour that it sort of floated in the air, lit up by a single Coleman lantern. Our mouths watered in anticipation of enjoying a slice of bread warmed up on the wood-fired stove. Idly I asked the nurses why there was so much flour on the loaves. One of the nurses looked at me and said, "Oh, that's not flour, that's dirt from the road. The gunny sacks were in the back of the truck and you know how dusty the road from La Paz is." We were not deterred. We ate it all.

The nursing missionaries' efforts to upgrade the health care of the local population met with limited success. Even with all the tuberculosis, it seemed their best outreach program was on the weekly market days when they set up a display of medical supplies on a blanket on the ground for the people to see and inquire about.

While we were visiting with the nurses, we saw firsthand the difficulty of receiving good medical attention when a young boy broke his shoulder playing soccer. First, his parents took him to a local medicine man, but after four days of his treatment, they finally agreed to send him to La Paz for treatment by a trained medial doctor. The boy had the ordeal of traveling by bus over the same bumpy, dusty road we had used to get there. Except with all the stops along the way, his trip took eight painful hours.

On Sundays we went to church. The parishioners walked to the church from miles around, so the service lasted for several hours in order to make it worth their while to attend. We, of course, were punctual; everyone else had the good sense to wander in at odd times. I can't tell you what a pleasure it was to sit there for hours on backless wooden benches watching a service that made very little sense. (It was spoken in Spanish and then translated into an obscure Indian dialect.) Occasionally there would be a hymn and we could recognize the tune, but never the words.

The women sat on one side of the church, the men on the other. The women took off their derby hats, while the men kept their brightly colored knit hats on. Dogs and cats wandered through the sanctuary. There was a full house, which was truly impressive given the distances they traveled on foot. The Methodist (we don't drink) Church had a rule that no one could join the church and continue to drink—or to dance, since dancing led to drinking.

While the native people were nominally Catholic, the Catholic Church did not have enough priests to have parishes in the area. The people were so starved for religion, for the word of God, that whole villages would convert to Methodism in order to have a church in which to worship. They would walk for miles and miles to come and worship. Upon their arrival, each person walked to the communion rail, knelt, and prayed before finding a seat. When church was over, they would walk those same miles back to the one-room adobe huts they called home. The homes had no windows because the climate was too cold to allow an opening. Nor did they have chimneys, so the smoke from their fires simply filtered through the thatched roofs. They went back to homes in which there were likely to be family members sick with tuberculosis; hence nearly 85 percent of the population had the debilitating disease. Theirs was a very tough existence.

So it was no wonder the local population liked to drink. We saw so many men walking around carrying gallon-sized purple cans that we became curious and finally one of us asked what was in the cans. The answer was alcohol. They would pour it into a car or an engine or down their own throats, whichever needed it more. The men would get so drunk that when they went fishing on the lake, they would throw dynamite to blow up schools of fish. Unfortunately, and all too frequently, they also blew off a hand or an arm. To curb drinking, the church banned dancing. Since a sign of a good party was the number of people passed out, parties with dancing were invitations to drunkenness. And because dancing led to drinking, the missionaries banned all dancing at parties. Personally, I was amazed anyone converted to Methodism.

One Wednesday evening, we drove to a little village for a mission outreach in which the preaching missionary spoke in someone's home. The one-room house was so crowded with people standing elbow to elbow, that there was no possibility of finding room to sit. And still there were people outside wanting to come in to hear him. Of course, it was Spanish translated into the Indian dialect again. I was unable to understand anything that was said, so I observed what was going on around us. As I stood there, I found myself looking up at the thatched roof expecting to see someone cutting a hole in the ceiling to lower a sick person into the room to be healed, just as it happened with Jesus in Capernaum. It was a humbling experience.

Not Quite the Peace Corps

Periodically I received letters from home. Mine crossed with Mother's in the mail. My letters were filled with accounts of the hardships we were enduring. Although I always ended my letters with the admonition "Don't worry about me, I'm fine," I knew in my heart Mother would worry, and that was fine. After all, that was her job.

Mother's letters were a tour de force of the *National Geographic*. "While you are in Bolivia," she would write, "you should be seeing women in derby hats, men in colorful knitted caps, and babies being carried on the backs of the women. The llamas are beasts of burden and are used for carrying provisions." The *National Geographic* did not lie to my mother. Everything was just as it should be.

We ended up building three outhouses. They named mine Loudell's Well. Obviously, there was some confusion about its use, but I'm proud to say I have a building named for me on the shores of Lake Titicaca.

When we left La Paz for Cochabamba, Bolivia, we took the same prop plane out. Because the air was so thin the takeoff went on forever, and then it seemed as if the pilot simply ran the plane off the edge of the mountain and let it drop and catch the wind—something like taking off from an aircraft carrier. Only this time the pilot didn't bother to pressurize the cabin. I guess he felt it wasn't really necessary since we were flying down to the plains of Bolivia. That flight was horrible. We all had terrible earaches and the poor babies on board screamed the entire trip. But Cochabamba was delightful. Its subtropical atmosphere was filled with color from brightly blooming flowers and shrubs. This was a wealthy city, and it offered us a welcome respite from sleeping on the floors and throwing water down those toilets. Eventually, we went to Chile, Argentina, and Brazil.

Wouldn't you know, after all my notions about Bible-toting missionaries, I was the one who ended up carrying the Bible under her arm. Now in my defense, after buying too much stuff to fit in the suitcase, I discovered that the Bible took up too much space. The first time I carried it with me, the customs agent took one look at it and passed me right along without checking my bags. After that, I always carried it when traveling through customs and it always worked. Praise the Lord.

CHAPTER TWO

HOW ON EARTH DID YOU GET THAT JOB?

*Life is 10 percent what happens to you and
90 percent how you react to it.*
—Charles R. Swindoll

During my senior year in college, a number of us in my sorority took advantage of a warm, sunny day in March to sunbathe on the deck. As I lay relaxing in the sun, I listened to the conversations swirling around me. The discussion was about marriage, the lack of good prospective husbands for several of them, and the urgency to find someone because graduation was looming.

To me, that seemed so premature. I wasn't ready to become a wife; there were things I hadn't yet learned that I knew would be important to know, such as how to cook or order fuel oil for the house I would one day have, and I still hadn't mastered balancing my checkbook. And there were probably lots of other things to learn before I could marry!

Several of the girls on the deck who had had no one in their sights that day were engaged by graduation. But I had other plans. I would work first, get married when I was twenty-five, and have my first child at twenty-seven and my second one at thirty.

When I shared that game plan with Mother, she admonished, "That's a fine plan, Loudell; just be careful. Life has a way of not working out the way you anticipate." I was young. I didn't heed her words.

In the third grade, I came to the first of many crossroads of my life. I needed to know right then what I was going to do with the rest of my life. So at dinner I asked Dad for advice. "Should I be a teacher or a nurse?" I asked. "Well," he replied with only a heartbeat of reflection, "if you become a nurse, you'll have to take out bedpans and give shots." So I decided to be a teacher, and that's all I wanted to be until the day I graduated from college. That's when I turned to my father and said, "I don't think I want to see the inside of a classroom again."

I had a teaching offer in Oakland, California, but Mother didn't want me to accept that position. She probably thought that was too far away, but I also suspect she felt it would look as if I were chasing after Paul, a friend who lived in Los Angeles, whom I had dated my junior year. That we would still be four hundred miles apart made no difference to her. Nothing would do but that I stay east of the Mississippi River. I applied late in the season to the Atlanta school system. On the application where it asked if I had any experience in the public health field, I said yes, I'd built outhouses in the Andes. I didn't hear from them.

By that time, in 1963, Phil and Jacquie, his bride of almost a year, were in Atlanta. I had thoughts of getting a job as a receptionist somewhere until the following year, when I might try for another teaching position. But Dad in his wisdom announced, "No man in his right mind would hire you at a living wage. I'll have to subsidize you, and if that is the case, then you will go to Katharine Gibbs Secretarial School in New York City." End of discussion.

I went to New York City kicking and screaming, probably because I was tired of school. But once there I did enjoy New York. How could I not? If I had studied as hard at college as I did at Katie Gibbs, I would never have ended up at Katie Gibbs.

Once again, the hand of God seemed to touch my shoulder and turned me in the direction it wanted me to go.

In the spring of 1964, after completing the Katie Gibbs course, I started looking for a place to live in New York as I began job hunting. One day while racing to catch a subway, I bumped into a well-dressed woman, causing her to drop several shopping bags. As I turned to look at her and her spilled bags, she looked at me to see if I was going to do the polite thing and help her gather her things together. I turned and continued on to the subway. Another train would have been coming in two minutes, but I didn't stop and help as I would have when I first arrived in the city. When I reflected on that as I rode home, I realized I didn't like how I acted; perhaps I should get out of New York before I became even more insensitive.

I went to Washington, DC, to visit Mary Beth Long, a childhood friend, and to check out the job scene. Spring arrived that weekend, and I was hooked. Washington is beautiful in the spring. We ended up sharing a furnished house in Georgetown with three other women. The house was on Thomas Jefferson Street, just three doors from the C&O Canal.

Wednesdays were my day to cook dinner. I had no clue what to do, having nearly flunked Foods 101 in college. No problem. My roommates all stood over me as I learned what sauté meant or what "adjust seasoning to taste" meant when you had no idea what it should taste like in the first place. They even had to teach me how to grocery shop—you start with the produce, which will be on the right when you enter the store, and so forth.

Politics—The Only Game in Town

When people learn I worked for Senator Edward Kennedy (EMK), they often ask how I got that job. It obviously was destiny, for surely I did nothing to help my cause.

My first job upon arriving in Washington in the spring of 1964 had been with the Pharmaceutical Manufacturers Association (PMA). When I didn't get the raise they promised at the end of my first year, I decided it was time to change jobs. Washington seemed to me to be a one-industry town—government. But I didn't want to work for some federal department for fear I would feel like just another cipher. Of the three branches of government, the Supreme Court seemed out of my league. I wasn't sure how to even approach the White House (notice I didn't consider other areas of the executive branch; it was the White House or nothing). So that left Congress. And since the Senate side seemed more important than the House side, that was obviously where I should be.

The Senate employment office representative asked me if I was a Democrat or a Republican. If I could have voted in the previous election I would probably have voted for Nixon, but I said I was registered to vote as a Democrat and wanted to work for a senator. She said the only Democratic senator needing a secretary was Senator Kennedy. He wanted a Katharine Gibbs-trained secretary who was a constituent. While I wasn't a constituent, I *was* Katie Gibbs-trained. What the heck, I applied. I told myself this was just for practice since I wasn't even sure I liked him. However, as I sat waiting for my interview during my lunch hour, I sized up the competition and thought I might have a chance. Hmm, maybe it would be interesting to work here after all.

The executive assistant who interviewed me asked me to return that day at six o'clock for an additional interview. I had thought this would be an after-hours interview, but when I arrived, the activity in the office convinced me this was definitely not after hours; the staff was still working at full throttle. The assistant took me into a large office and paused to chat with me for a moment or two while a man and woman finished their discussion at the other end of the room. Then the man walked forward with the help of a cane. It was Senator Kennedy. He was gorgeous, as in mind-numbing, matinee-idol gorgeous. As he directed me to a seat on the sofa and returned to sit behind his desk, I recalled that he had only recently returned to work after breaking his back in a deadly plane crash the year before.

Katharine Gibbs prides itself on preparing their secretaries to handle job interviews. If they had heard this interview, they would have snatched away my diploma. The senator quickly perused my résumé and in a nonthreatening manner that was rather pleasant, began asking me questions; I assured him I liked whatever he asked about.

"I see you graduated from Katharine Gibbs's school in New York City. Did you enjoy Katie Gibbs?"

"Yes, I did."

"Now you are working for the Pharmaceutical Manufacturers Association?"

"Yes, I am."

"Do you like working at the Pharmaceutical Manufacturers Association?"

"Yes, I do."

It would have been nice to have elaborated on *any* of those questions, but my mind was too numb. And so, it went until he asked what I did at PMA. I looked off to gather my thoughts and spied a framed painting on his wall. It looked like a child's finger painting, but could it be a Picasso? While I was considering this perplexing question, I heard myself begin to answer his question, so I tuned in to hear what I was saying.

To my horror I heard, "Well, I deliver the mail."

I stopped right there and then and said, "No, I don't. I don't know why I would say something like that, because I certainly don't deliver the mail. The mail is delivered to me. I open it and give it to my boss."

Eventually the ordeal was over. As I stood to leave, he rose and escorted me to the door, leaning a bit on his cane. I tried to rally my forces when he asked me one last basic question: "Where do you live?"

I replied, "I live in Georgetown, but I'll soon be moving into an apartment on Tunlaw Road with a friend from college who lives across the street from you." Then in an effort to forge some kind of collegiality with him through my soon-to-be roommate, I added, "As a matter of fact, she's one of the girls who live in the house on the corner across from you."

Have you ever heard the term "icicles dripped from every word he said"? Well, I looked for them because the senator's words hung in the air when he replied, "Oh, *those* girls. They crashed my party." And *then* I remembered the huge guffaw Washington had had at his expense when some young women who lived across the street from him dressed up in evening gowns and crashed his very elite party.

Well, that was certainly a fine interview. After a disaster like that, there was nothing to do but to move on. While at home for a weekend visit, sitting on the patio having a drink, I told Dad I had interviewed for a new job. Thought I would work on Capitol Hill. Actually, I had interviewed for a position with Ted Kennedy. He was stunned.

"Elinor! Come, hear what Loudell has done!"

Something I've learned over the years is that parents never really think their kids can do anything without their help. So he turned to me and said, "Let me think. Oh, dear, I don't know anyone who could help you get that position. That's a new field for me. I can't help you," he bemoaned despondently. I hope I had the presence of mind, as well as the graciousness, to say that he had already helped me by giving me the education I needed for the job. I do know I sat there and basked in the glory of their wonder that I had had the nerve to even try for the position.

Eventually I lowered my standards and interviewed with a Georgia congressman. That job interview was rather short and sweet, certainly nothing memorable. The only reason I can give for even considering a position on the House side is that, by then, I'd been at this job hunting for almost a month and I was desperate. Well, not desperate so much as tired of the waiting. After all was said and done, however, I'd interviewed with all of two people, Ted Kennedy and the Georgia congressman.

So I took a week-long vacation in Ocean City with some friends. There we soaked up some sun, enjoyed the nightlife, and talked about men. We were halfway through our week when my roommate called to say I had received a telegram. It read, "Unable to reach you by phone, please call me." It was signed by the executive assistant to Senator Kennedy.

Obviously, they wanted to hire me. Not so fast, if you please.

I called the executive assistant for the Georgia congressman first and asked him how my interview had gone, and what my chances of getting the position were. I explained that I needed to know this because I probably had a job offer from Senator Kennedy. He replied that my chances with the congressman weren't good, but if he could give me some advice it would be to grab the job with Senator Kennedy as fast as I could. So I did. And then I called my boss at PMA and gave notice. I offered to cut my vacation short and return to work, but he said to stay and enjoy myself. Then I called my father; he was stunned.

(After what I considered a disaster of an interview, I've always thought what probably happened was that it had been so long since my meeting with Senator Kennedy he forgot who I was.) I was so excited about the job I even forgot to ask what my pay would be. Thank heavens it was five dollars a week more than I was paid at PMA.

The atmosphere on the Hill was entirely different from my previous job. There was much more energy. Personal initiative was the hallmark for everyone. Cramped quarters were standard fare. And a sense of purpose permeated the senator's office. For someone who had been all nerves at her interview, I was remarkably calm on my first day of work. Even so I was startled when, with no forewarning, certainly no mention in the interview of what I would be doing, I was handed a law book, a short list of contacts and their phone numbers in various departments of government, and a pile of mail, and was then declared to be the new immigration caseworker. The outgoing caseworker, who should have spent a week showing me how to handle the workload, gave me a day, and then she was off to the senator's legislative office for her new and more exciting secretarial position.

It turned out my new job was to solve any immigration problems the senator's constituents might have. That night I took the law book home, curled up in bed, and read and highlighted passages of the United

States immigration law. Massachusetts really does have a great diversity of ethnic backgrounds, and the immigrants didn't hesitate to ask for help. Usually, it simply boiled down to helping expedite paperwork in some agency or checking into their problems and writing letters for the senator's signature, which was applied by a machine. But two cases really stood out.

A recent immigrant couple from Greece had to leave their young son, who was diagnosed with grand mal epilepsy, behind when they came to the United States. People with petite mal were acceptable, but apparently not those with grand mal seizures. The parents had physicians and hospitals lined up to take care of their son, if only there were some way to get him here. *Could the senator help?*

I called my contact at the Department of Health, and together we came up with the idea to send the surgeon general of the United States, who was going to Paris for a speech, on a detour to Athens, have him check out the boy, and change the diagnosis to petite mal. And that's what he did so the child could come to live with his parents in America.

In the second case, with the Cold War at its height, a Hungarian mother and son were using their vacation in Yugoslavia as an opportunity to flee to America. They had a US visa, but it was only good if they could get to Switzerland. They couldn't get an exit visa from Yugoslavia, and their exit visa from Hungry that permitted them to travel to Yugoslavia would soon expire. When they returned to Hungary, their chance to come to America would be gone. *Could the senator help?*

Well, we sent letters and calls and telegrams to the State Department and to the American Embassy in Belgrade and, while everyone was sympathetic, it still came down to getting that exit visa from Yugoslavia, and that was not forthcoming. I discovered later that, when all else had failed, our people at the American Embassy smuggled the mother and son out of the country in the trunk of a car.

Working Hard, Playing Hard

Our office was a suite of five rooms with high ceilings, ten or twelve feet high. One entered the reception area of what would have been room number two in the series of five rooms. The room to the left of the receptionist, room number one, held other secretaries and caseworkers. The senator's personal secretary, the appointment secretary, and his administrative assistant were in the room to the right of the reception area, or room number three; next was the senator's private office, room number four; and on the other side of him in room number five was the legislative office.

Space was so limited that our desks abutted each other; not even enough room for those half-walled dividers so loved by corporations today. Once in my early days there, the senator had an "efficiency expert" look at the offices to reconfigure our spaces. After studying it a bit, he declared there should be a minimum of three to four feet of personal space around each individual; in other words, double the space we had. He said the only office approaching his parameters was the legislative office. We puzzled over that for a while until it dawned on us he had been there at lunchtime when half the people were in the cafeteria. What the heck, we were fine as we were.

The senator's office was a long room with doors in the front and rear that led to the legislative office, one in the front that led to his secretary's office, and a fourth door that led to the outside hallway. If he needed to enter his office without going through the reception area, this was an ideal way. In the old Senate Office Building, his office had a fireplace, as did the other senators' offices. The room was plenty large enough for a sofa on the wall and chairs grouped around the fireplace.

My office was a room down the hall and around the corner from the main office. Besides me, there was Dick Drayne, the senator's press secretary; someone who opened the mail and handled the military casework; an AP teletype in the corner, so Dick could have instant access to any news that might need a quick response; and next to that was a mimeograph machine for printing news releases and copies of speeches. I think one other person eventually had a desk in the office, plus we had the autopen, a machine used to sign the senator's name to letters.

It wasn't long after I began working for Senator Kennedy that I proudly took my parents to see the offices. It was a Sunday and no one was there, so we wandered around and ended up in the senator's office, looking at his memorabilia, when who should walk in but the senator himself. After years of Mother's conscientious etiquette training, my proud parents stood there waiting for me to introduce them to my employer, the celebrated senator from Massachusetts. My intention was to introduce them as Phil and Elinor Insley, but as I turned to do so and looked them in the eye, I couldn't remember their names. I just stared at them as my mind went blank. They looked at me and waited. I turned to the senator and he was waiting. Everyone waited while I tried to remember my own parents' names! Frantically I thought, *What is my name?* And I came up with Loudell Insley. Yes! "Senator Kennedy, I would like for you to meet my parents, Dr. and Mrs. Insley." Thank God I wasn't married!

The senator was most gracious. He took over the tour and since we were standing in front of the fireplace in his office he began by unfurling his older brother's presidential flag, which is blue with the presidential seal. This was the one that had been displayed beside President Kennedy's (JFK's) casket as he lay in state in the White House following his assassination only two years earlier. On the other side of the fireplace was an American flag. It had been flying over the

Capitol on November 22, when his brother had been killed. He also showed off his daughter's finger painting (which turned out not to be a Picasso), and chatted with us for a while before we took our leave. Mother and Dad said they were impressed.

Once I got the hang of the immigration work, it wasn't long before I was also helping Dick. That was the fun stuff—working on speeches, meeting the press, being involved with legislation. I loved it.

It also got me out of the office some, running press releases to the press room in the Senate, picking up the papers at the airport that were flown in each day from Boston. (Parking was at such a premium near the office building that I often used the senator's car since he had a parking permit.) There were some really nice reporters that covered the Massachusetts delegation—Matt Storin, Dick Stewart, Marty Nolan. There wasn't much stress doing both immigration work and helping Dick. Occasionally we'd work until seven or eight o'clock on a speech that needed editing and mimeographing.

When I began working for Ted Kennedy in the spring of 1965, his older brother, Robert Kennedy (RFK), had begun his term as senator from New York that January. Ted Kennedy was junior to Robert Kennedy in age, but he was his senior in the US Senate, having finished his older brother's Senate term when he was elected president. That fall he had been reelected to his own full term while lying flat on his broken back in a Boston hospital. But all the excitement about the Kennedys centered on Robert Kennedy. The press, the public, everyone wanted to know what he was thinking, doing, going to do. As the youngest brother, EMK may have had the Kennedy mystique, but at that time he didn't have much stature with the press or the public.

With the spotlight aimed at his brother, he had the luxury of relative peace and quiet. Ted Kennedy worked hard, and he worked his staff hard. And he educated himself. He took courses on subjects of interest to him, and he read voraciously—the Library of Congress was at his beck and call. It seemed as if books from the library were being constantly shuffled back and forth as if on a conveyer belt. Unlike other senators, after reading a particularly insightful book, he would invite the author to meet with him so he could discuss the subject in more depth. If he was out of town, even in Europe, we would send him a briefcase stuffed with memos, drafts of bills and speeches, and letters for his review and/or signature. The briefcase would be handed to an airline pilot who would deliver it to an aide at the other end of the line. In a few days it would be returned with everything marked up. I have always felt that if all our senators and congressmen worked as hard as he did, regardless of which side of an issue they were on, the country would be much better off.

Eventually the senator was invited to appear on the television show *Meet the Press*. The staff hummed with excitement. It was his first appearance as a senator and we all wanted to be in the audience to give him support. Naturally we should have a party afterward. After much discussion and comparison of driving distances from the studio to various people's homes, it was decided that the party should be at my apartment—the one I shared with Judy Schaeffer, one of the girls who had lived in the house across the street from the senator when his party was crashed. What symmetry! Both the television interview and the party were a success; as it turned out, that was the first of many parties I would give.

Ted Kennedy was absolutely loyal to his brother and of course his brother was to him.

Robert Kennedy's staff looked down their noses at us, however, and we reciprocated. There would be subtle little jabs, such as referring to our boss as Teddy, instead of Senator Kennedy, or asking with a raised eyebrow, "Oh, is that what Teddy said?" as if he were out of the loop on something.

We may have worked hard, but we played hard too, especially if we were competing with Robert Kennedy's office. There was a touch football league on the Hill and of course both brothers' offices were in it. We played on the most beautiful football field in the world, the Washington ellipse, with the Washington Monument and the White House at the end zones and the Lincoln Memorial and the Capitol of the United States on the sidelines.

The teams were eight members, three of whom had to be women, but that didn't slow down the games. No one gave any quarter. During one of the games, I got an elbow in the mouth and lost a tooth.

By the time our teams played each other, we were fighting for the championship. The tension was high and the stakes were even higher. Even the press couldn't resist stopping by to cover the game. Later that evening Robert Kennedy, who was touring Peru at the time, checked in with his office to find out the results. They lost, we won, and it was wonderful.

The entire time I worked on the Hill, I constantly reminded myself to appreciate all I was a part of. History was being made and I had a view, not from the front row seats, but even better, from the wings, with one eye on the stage and a hand behind the curtain, helping the principals play their roles. Therefore, I was seeing not just the public persona with the bright smile ready to be the person the public expected and wanted, I was there to see the exhaustion or uncertainty. Occasionally, in a small way, I was there to help choose which face a potentially historic figure should show the world. It was heady stuff.

At cocktail parties, people actually listened to what I said when I enthusiastically shared the dirt that such-and-such bill would never pass because it was dead in committee since the chairman hated the bill's sponsor and would never let it come to a vote. Or I would observe that a particular piece of legislation was getting marked up in committee so much that its own mother wouldn't recognize it. I was so wise and sophisticated. I was enjoying myself immensely.

My family was not so impressed by my position. My brother was certainly not. He would call and shout at me, "Have you seen what your senator has done this time!?"

Acting as if it were a family scandal, our cousin, Anne Phillips, who was visiting Phil and Jacquie in Baltimore at the time and was alone in the house with Jacquie, moved from her seat across the room to sit next to Jacquie on the sofa. Then she whispered in scandalized sympathy, "Is Loudell still working for Senator Kennedy?"

Small towns tend to be conservative by nature, at least mine is. Rumors travel with the speed of light there, and as a child I discovered that fact the hard way. I had casually mentioned to a friend, as kids will do, that Dad might be called up to serve in the Korean War. He wasn't, but his practice fell off dramatically. Not until a patient mentioned she would miss him when he went into the service did he finally figure out the problem—and the culprit. So with that in mind, my parents were careful about what appeared in our newspaper.

Our hometown paper, the *Daily Times*, had a little society column that printed brief items, such as: so-and-so had just returned from vacationing in Florida, or so-and-so's sister was visiting from Philadelphia. When Helen Perry, the columnist, asked Mother if she could print that I was home visiting from Washington, DC, where I worked for Senator Kennedy, Mother exclaimed, "Heavens, no! Don't ever put *that* in print." It may have been an honor to have her daughter working for the Kennedys, but let's not *publish* the fact. Who knew what his patients' reactions might be?

While my family and friends back home were horrified at how liberal I had become, in the office I was the conservative. Dick asked me to come back from Salisbury one weekend to help with a speech the senator was giving to the Southern Christian Leadership Conference (SCLC, an African-American civil rights organization). I of course jumped at the chance to be involved. For some reason my opinion of the speech seemed to be important to Dick, and I was happy to give it.

When Dick asked what I thought after the first draft, I said, "The senator is one of the few white people who could address this conference at this time and actually be listened to. He should make this speech less saccharine and more substantive, more what they really need to hear."

Dick took it off to the other speechwriters and apparently gave them my feedback, for he later came back with a draft that was stronger. When he asked if I was satisfied now, I said "Well, it's better, but still not very strong." Off he went. Next came another complete revision. It was better, but not great. So back to the trenches once again. And so it went all day, until finally time ran out. The senator had to catch his plane.

Amid the background of the New England accents and their occasional liberal indignation, my little bit of a southern accent sometimes reminded staff that I was just a little bit different. This seemed to be one of those times. Dick looked at me and with a quirky smile asked what others in the office had often asked, "Now, once again, just how was it you got hired?"

The next day, however, he came in with yet another revision of the speech. The senator, while flying to Atlanta, had revised it again and made it even tougher. "Now are you happy?" Dick asked. "Yes, that's finally much better," I declared, giving it my personal stamp of approval!

As family of a slain president, the senator was invited to a number of functions honoring his brother, and when he could, he included his staff. The Naval Academy had a sailing regatta honoring President Kennedy and of course the senator, a sailing enthusiast, was invited. Any of us who wished to could join him—as usual, no dates, only spouses. Naturally I went. I brought the Bloody Marys. The problem with a sailboat is that it tilts! That alarmed me but didn't prevent my going—hence the drinks!

When the *John F. Kennedy* aircraft carrier was christened in May of 1967, our whole staff was invited. Christening a new ship is a big deal. With a naval band playing wonderful military music, how could one not feel the pride of being an American? The speeches were mercifully short. And then the president's family, Jackie, Caroline, and John Jr., moved to the bow of the ship and Caroline cracked the bottle of champagne against the hull and the ship slipped safely into the water and didn't sink—always a good thing. There were refreshments in a huge building dockside and then the event was over, for most of the people.

Of course, I had additional plans. Time-wise the return trip from Norfolk to DC was about the same whether one returned the way we had driven from Washington or if we returned by driving up the eastern shore of Maryland, through Salisbury! So I invited the office staff to lunch at my parents' home, which was on the way. It was a sign of the times that my directions to the house were very simple: cross the Chesapeake Bay Bridge-Tunnel, turn left at the third stoplight (a hundred miles away), turn right at the next light, and our house will be about five blocks north. (Nowadays the same dual-lane road has many, many more stoplights.)

Because of Robert Kennedy's crusade for migrant workers' rights, our office was very sensitive about these issues, and since our farmers on the shore used migrant labor, all my friends' eyes had apparently been eager to see them at work. Alas, it was the wrong time of the year, and there were none. But when they arrived at my home, they asked if the many long, low houses they had seen along the way were houses for the migrant workers.

"Heavens, no," I joked, "those are chicken houses. We wouldn't have anything that good for migrant workers." (The fact is I don't recall ever seeing any migrant worker camps.)

As I learned my way around my little world on the Hill, I acquired the self-confidence and sophistication that comes from the personal, deep-down knowledge that you have your act together and are definitely hot stuff. This notion was reinforced by the attention I received from people in high places.

For example, when Republican Senator Percy was first elected, his temporary offices were across the hall from ours, and he would frequently pop into our office for a visit and shoot the breeze with us after office hours. He was a rising star in the newly elected Republican class of senators, and we were delighted he would choose to simply sit on the edge of a desk and chitchat about nothing in particular—but at the same time we all knew we were each sizing up the other for future political maneuvers.

Senator Hollings was always the gentleman, and if he saw me carrying a heavy load—my suitcase or a stack of newspapers—he would say, "Here let me help you with that," and grab whatever it was and carry it to the office for me. He had those smooth southern manners that came very naturally to him but were generally ingratiating to the recipient. Certainly so for me.

My Republican congressman's brother, Senator Thurston Morton, had his office near mine. Though he rarely spoke (he was often just a little tight), he would usually nod a dignified greeting to me as he made his way to his office. Now that I think about it, that was usually after lunch, and who am I to throw stones?

Senator Inouye's office was also across the hall from my office around the corner. One day his aide stuck his head in the door and asked me to lunch. I had seen him frequently in the hallway and had nodded or spoken to him in passing, so I was delighted to have a lunch date with him. It was a beautiful spring day, and I was happy to be out in the fresh air as we walked the couple blocks to the restaurant.

Not far from us a solitary man walked along with a stiffness that seemed overly careful. "Oh, there goes Senator John Tower, drunk again," my friend said derisively. (That reputation would haunt him years later when President George Bush nominated him to be Secretary of Defense, and he was not confirmed by his fellow senators.)

We went to the Monocle, *the* restaurant on the Hill. It wasn't the first time I'd been there for lunch, but it was the first time I hadn't actually eaten lunch there; instead, I had several gin gimlets for lunch (three-martini lunches were the "in thing" then), when I realized it was late and I needed to get back to work.

As we walked back to the office, he whispered in my ear, "I love pussy, don't you? I mean I could eat some pussy right now. Want to have some pussy?"

I looked him straight in the eye and declared in my most self-righteous voice, "Heavens, no, I'm allergic to cats. I have been since I was twenty-one." I continued walking. He stopped dead in his tracks. Okay, I guess I wasn't as sophisticated as I thought.

CHAPTER THREE

INSIDE A PRESIDENTIAL CAMPAIGN

Idealists, foolish enough to throw caution to the winds, have advancedmankind and have enriched the world.
—Anonymous

I saw a different world one day when I delivered some papers to Robert Kennedy's office, which was in the new Senate Office Building across the street from us. The phones were jangling off the hook, people were rushing in and out of his offices, tourists were loitering in the hall hoping to see the senator "just to shake his hand," people with appointments were waiting, photographers and the press were waiting, and aides were walking and talking with colleagues as they rushed to appointments. There was electricity in the air. The presidential primaries were warming up, and surely Robert Kennedy would soon be announcing his decision to run. It seemed everyone wanted to be in on the action.

However, Robert Kennedy surprised everyone when he reluctantly announced he would not be running for president in the 1968 primaries. An antiwar liberal, Eugene McCarthy, picked up the cause, ran and made an impressive showing against President Johnson in the New Hampshire primary. Bobby reconsidered *his* decision and finally announced on March 16, 1968, that he would be seeking the presidency. Then Lyndon Johnson announced shortly thereafter that he would *not* be seeking reelection. You needed a program just to keep track of the players and their positions.

Robert Kennedy may have had many reasons for not throwing his hat into the ring before the New Hampshire primary, but it was McCarthy who had shown how weak President Johnson was—that he could be beaten. That hesitation cost Bobby Kennedy dearly. Gene McCarthy stole the hearts and souls of the young people with his courageous decision to defy the establishment. And the young people stuck with their new standard bearer, even after their longtime champion entered the fray. They even cut their hair, cleaned up their acts, and became Clean for Gene, a very big deal for some of them. Then they knocked on doors, held rallies, sent out mailers and worked their hearts out for their man. They were an army working against us and for McCarthy.

Gene McCarthy had a good, solid head start when Robert Kennedy launched his bid. So he had a lot of ground to cover just to catch up to his opponent. But he had a not-so-secret weapon, the Kennedy Machine.

You've heard the expression, "They seemed to come out of the woodwork." Robert Kennedy's campaign headquarters, set up in an office in downtown Washington, DC, exemplified this. Telegrams began pouring in from John F. Kennedy's campaign workers. One would say, "I handled Jack's travel desk, I'll be there to help Bobby on Tuesday." Another might say, "I'll be there next week to handle acquiring furnishings." Yet others volunteered for nearly everything that a campaign could need—somewhere someone had already done that for Robert Kennedy's brother and was willing to pack up and move to DC to help in the next campaign. It was, indeed, the Kennedy Machine.

Fortunately, it didn't take me long to get transferred to the campaign, where all the action was. The press office had RFK's press secretary, Frank Mankiewicz; EMK's press secretary, Dick Drayne; and JFK's press secretary, Pierre Salinger. Since this made it a little top-heavy, Frank eventually went to California to work on the campaign there, Dick traveled with the candidate, and Pierre remained at the headquarters to handle things there. Lucky Pierre had me to help him.

Located upstairs, the power players, along with the "Boiler Room," were supervised by RFK's best friend and college roommate, Dave Hackett. The Boiler Room girls were Nance Lyons, Mary Ellen Lyons, Mary Jo Kopechne, Esther Newberg, Susan Tannenbaum, and Rosemary (Cricket) Keogh. The Boiler Room was so called because it was a high-pressure operation. They worked really long hours and were vitally important to the cause. In the Democratic Party at that time, unlike now, nearly half of the delegates would *not* be selected by primary vote, but by appointments and caucuses. Thus it was important to gather those delegates into the fold. RFK's opponent for the nomination, Eugene McCarthy, had captured the younger voters' interest, the voters who really should have been supporting Robert Kennedy and would have been had he not dithered about running—and now RFK had his work cut out for him.

The girls' jobs were to learn everything there was to know about their assigned states: the power brokers, the money people, volunteers, precinct leaders, newspaper editors, all the politicians at every level of government, and everything about their spouses and children—including names, birthdates, anniversaries, what teams the kids played on, what organizations everyone belonged to, and every other little thing that could possibly be helpful at a future date. Of course, they also had to be aware of all local and state issues and topics, such as what teams were playing, where, and whether they were winning or losing—all of this information had to be kept updated.

When the candidate went to a Boiler Room girl's assigned state or town, she girl would feed him all the information so that he could know what to discuss and how to personalize his conversation with the individuals he met. In crucial states he would get a daily list of people to call and schmooze.

Not long into the campaign, I was sent to the Indianapolis campaign headquarters to work, to do anything that needed to be done. The political headquarters of a major candidate is a busy place. Add to it that Indiana was the first primary state Robert Kennedy was actually running in, and the action became even more intense. Here there was tons of activity with the national press stopping in to check things out, politicians jockeying for position, and volunteers running around. This was definitely where the excitement was. Here was the action. Boy, oh boy, this was going to be great.

I don't remember the offices too well, but I do recall the controlled chaos. It wasn't much different from Robert Kennedy's senate office. People were coming and going, the phones were ringing and the receptionist was trying to hold down the fort almost single-handedly. She had a desk in front of a barrier of some kind; as I think back on it, it could have been as simple as a curtain. There was a great deal to keep track of, and she appeared to be handling it like a veteran.

Unfortunately, I didn't linger long at headquarters. I was quickly shuffled off to a supporter's office where a bank of typewriters was set up for volunteers to type envelopes. Any organization is at the mercy of volunteers' schedules and whims. So there was more work than people to do it—and there I sat doing grunt work for days on end as the volunteers came and went.

At night I would drag myself back to my hotel for a bite to eat and then fall into bed. However, as I waited at the curb for a cab or bus one evening, Ted Kennedy, Dave Burke, the senator's chief of staff, and Jack Crimmins, his driver, were leaving the offices. The senator walked over and said they were going up the street for a hot dog; would I like to join them?

I'd like to think I simply answered, "Sure." After all, I'd been working for him for three years. But I'm afraid I hemmed and hawed for a moment before saying yes. I couldn't believe they really wanted me to join them. Well, the hot dog turned out to be at the most expensive restaurant in town. Of course we had the most visible table there.

Our waiter began by asking me if I wanted a drink, which I declined. When he asked what I wanted for dinner, I chose something very modest, like chicken. I had learned very early from Dad not to order the most expensive thing on the menu. But when Jack and the senator ordered a drink and filet mignon, I regrouped, remembering that I was with a millionaire. I called the waiter back and upped the ante. Dave gave me a knowing little smirk as he ordered milk toast.

The senator never carried cash, so when the bill was delivered to him, I wondered how he would handle it. It was impressive to see him boldly sign his name to the bill and then get up and leave. No identification needed, no billing address added, no credit card, just his name.

Later that evening Dick called me at my hotel and said he needed help, and that I should come over to his hotel and bring an overnight bag with a change of clothes. As I walked out of my hotel at midnight with my little overnight case, I wondered what the doorman was thinking. Then I mentally shook myself: *You don't need to wonder, you know exactly what he's thinking. Oh, well, I won't be seeing him again, so who cares?*

At the candidate's hotel we pulled an all-nighter, working on an important speech with RFK's speechwriter, Adam Walinsky. One doesn't simply sit down and pound out a speech. A presidential candidate needs a position on many issues—some of which can be brand-new to him, but vitally urgent to the voters in a particular state. Farm issues may not have seemed important to a New York senator, but they were a big deal in the Midwest, so they became important to a presidential candidate. Adam had some policy thinking to do. That takes time and effort. What if we do this? Or that? Didn't we say something about farming in a speech a few months ago, could we use some of that? There were no computers, so most of the research at two in the morning is done in the speechwriter's own head. So Adam dictated and I typed. We discarded some parts, moved other parts, retyped it all to see how that worked. Does it flow properly? This was becoming the candidate's farm policy. *Does it make sense?*

Meanwhile, Dick was trying to come up with some opening jokes. Alan King, a popular comedian, had generously provided opening lines for Ted Kennedy for years until once or twice Dick had filled in when King was too busy. Dick's jokes were good, so he eventually became the joke writer. It's not easy to create a new joke, particularly for someone else to deliver. They were always about the senator—at his expense, or perhaps about his family, or later he would play with his audiences about whether he was thinking of running for president.

But now, Dick was called on for big-time work for a presidential candidate on the stump. They had to be good. So he would sit at his typewriter thinking; there would be a spurt of typing, a pause, a chuckle, and then he'd pull the paper out of the typewriter and hand it to me. Most times they were good, and I'd laugh. Sometimes I'd hand it back and tell him to keep working. But if it was *really* good, I knew it because he'd yank it from the machine and with a big smile walk it over to someone else and share it.

The next day, Dick suggested I return to Washington with the campaign staff on the candidate's plane, perhaps my only chance to have such an experience. His last words to me as I boarded were, "Just don't sit up front; stay in the back and be invisible." It was so exciting. A friend and political reporter asked me to sit with him, but when Robert Kennedy boarded the plane and glared at me, I realized the fourth row was probably a touch too far forward, and I was definitely not invisible. Not good.

Suddenly the cabin darkened. What had happened? I looked at the door. It was pitch black. Rosey Grier, All-Pro defensive tackle, formerly of the Los Angeles Rams' Fearsome Foursome, and currently providing security for the candidate, was boarding the plane. His massive body blocked out all the sunlight. Behind him came Rafer Johnson, Olympic decathlon winner, also on the security detail, as was ex-FBI agent and family friend, Bill Barry. That was some impressive muscle protecting the senator. No one in his right mind would mess with them.

Unfortunately, since Robert Kennedy had spotted me sitting too far forward in the plane and not being the invisible staffer the Kennedys preferred, I was grounded when we reached Washington. Of course, being at headquarters wasn't so bad, but I now had a taste of being on the road, and that was where I wanted to be.

A few days after my return, Dick Harwood of the *Washington Post* called Pierre Salinger at the DC office looking for a response to an article he was writing for the next day's edition. He was going to tell about his experience when he stopped by our Indianapolis headquarters and was mistaken for a local politician. Thinking he was there to pick up his "walking-around money," our busy receptionist had handed him an envelope with a lot of cash. Walking-around money was used for either getting out the vote or for getting the judges to look the other way at the polls when our get-out-the-vote efforts arrived at the polls, whichever was needed. Did we have a comment? Unfortunately, Pierre wasn't there, only me. I offered to find him, but there wasn't time. Dick was on deadline. So the story ran with no softening comments from the Kennedy campaign. The story never got much play because other events caught up with us.

A few days later, about three weeks into the campaign, all hell broke loose.

Dick had popped out for a quick dinner and I was alone in the office when the AP wire began signaling a major story. Checking the wire, I found to my horror Martin Luther King Jr. had been assassinated. It wasn't long before riots broke out throughout the country. Robert Kennedy was in Indianapolis when he heard the news and it was he who first announced Dr. King's death to a black audience. It was a remarkable extemporaneous speech. He spoke about the pain of death, which everyone knew he spoke of from agonizingly personal experience. As he spoke, he quoted from memory something that was obviously etched deep into his own heart:

My favorite poet was Aeschylus. He wrote: "In our sleep, pain which cannot forget falls drop by drop upon the heart until, in our own despair, against our will, comes wisdom through the awful grace of God."

(Historians rank that six-minute speech as one of the great American speeches of the twentieth century. Many major cities had riots and significant fires that weekend, but not Indianapolis. Robert Kennedy's speech is credited for helping to keep that city calm.)

Then he flew home to Washington, where the city was burning.

I was at the campaign headquarters when a curfew was announced, and I wasn't about to leave the action to go home and huddle in my apartment all alone, so I stayed and worked. Several areas of town were on fire. It was alarming to see armed soldiers in battle dress circling our national buildings, prepared for an attack. The National Guard surrounded the White House and the Capitol, guns at the ready; they patrolled the streets in jeeps, and curfew was strictly enforced. Washington resembled a city under siege.

Dick and I were among the last to leave headquarters. It was late when we closed up shop and much too dangerous for me to drive home alone, so I followed Dick to his house and slept on his sofa. The next day, Friday, I drove to my apartment with my headlights on to show sympathy for Martin Luther King Jr.—and to keep from being attacked by roaming bands of troublemakers. My apartment building, however, was in southeast Washington, just around the block from Vice President Hubert Humphrey's condo. So the police patrolled there constantly. It was extremely quiet.

In the afternoon Phil and Jacquie called, concerned for my safety. They urged me to come to Baltimore where it was safer. Of course, I had forgotten to turn off the lights on my car so the battery had died and no one would come to service my car during a riot. But in one of life's little miracles, the battery recharged itself with some rest, and I went to Baltimore, even though it, too, had erupted into rioting. Baltimore is only an hour's drive from Washington and the traffic was rather thin on the highway with most people staying home in front of their TV sets. I stayed there through Saturday, but like a moth drawn to the flame, I couldn't stay away from the campaign for long, so I returned to DC late Sunday afternoon.

Sunday, in an effort to calm the city, Robert Kennedy went to a black Baptist church in Washington to worship. Communion was served and he participated. Well, we spent Monday cleaning up that mess, searching for a Jesuit priest who was liberal enough to affirm that it was okay for Senator Kennedy to accept communion in a Protestant church. The campaign was put on hold until Martin Luther King Jr. was laid to rest.

Dick went back on the campaign trail and I stayed in town. One day he called and said he'd just returned and was exhausted. He needed to get to Atlantic City, where the candidate was to speak, and then Dick would catch the campaign's charter plane back to DC. Could I drive him in his car to Atlantic City, spend the night, and then drive myself back? Naturally I said yes.

I picked him up after work around seven or eight o'clock, and off we went. Well, I was so engrossed in hearing the news about the campaign that I took a small wrong turn and ended up in Virginia! We reached Atlantic City much later than we had expected. We had no hotel reservations and very little cash between us, so we stayed in some cheap motel. Two rooms, of course!

Credit cards were not that common then and I didn't have one. So the next day Dick gave me his card to buy gas, and I headed for home. Would you believe I lost the card? I wasn't used to credit cards, and when the service station attendant brought me the credit card slip to sign with the card stuck in his new little tray, we both overlooked it, and off I drove. When I realized what I had done several hours later I tried to call the gas attendant. My luck was holding. It was a new station; the unions had struck the phone company, therefore the station had no telephone service.

In spite of that, when I reached Dick's home later that day he told me Angie Novello, Robert Kennedy's personal secretary, had had a death in her family and would have to leave the campaign trail for a week. Did I want to fill in until she could return? If so, we had to be at the plane within the hour. It wouldn't wait for us so I would need to go home, pack a bag, pick up Dick at the Senate Office Building, and then get us to the airport on time. Amazing what you can do with the proper motivation.

Aboard the campaign plane, the candidate sat in what would have been the first-class section. The staff and press (who paid their own way, which helped to defray the cost to the campaign for chartering the plane) sat in what would have been economy class. Two tables had been installed in the rear of the plane with IBM Selectric typewriters attached to them so we could type materials, such as speeches and press releases, while we flew. This time I made sure I was well back in the plane.

Just before takeoff, a Secret Service agent arrived carrying a package and handed it to Carol Welch, one of the three traveling secretaries on the flight. Jackie Kennedy had sent a full Thermos of Tiger's Milk, along with a travel case containing a miniature blender, ingredients, and a handwritten recipe for making more. Apparently, this was energy food that Jack Kennedy had found to be invigorating while on his presidential campaign, and she thought Bobby might find it helpful. The ingredients included yeast, wheat germ, and other stuff that didn't look too appetizing; who knew about health food in those days? We never gave the senator any of it. Eventually the Thermos with the yeast in it exploded in his suitcase. What a wonderful surprise to open his bag and find all his clothes soaked with Jackie's Tiger's Milk. We quickly sent everything to the hotel laundry for a rush job. I just wish I had had the presence of mind to get Jackie's handwritten recipe card before someone else did.

When we arrived in Lincoln, Nebraska, at midnight there was a crowd waiting at the airport. While Bobby worked the ropes, we unloaded the plane. Heaven forbid we should have our stuff stowed in the hold where someone else could handle it for us; no, we kept it topside where we could reach everything, and therefore we had to load it ourselves every time we flew.

Our baggage consisted of three portable manual typewriters, a manual speech typewriter (large font), a portable mimeograph machine, a footlocker trunk full of supplies, a new thing called a fax machine (which was the size of a small suitcase but weighed a ton), Jeff Greenfield's guitar so he could strum while he composed speeches, suitcases for each of us (there were at least nine staff traveling with the candidate), Jackie Kennedy's little case, Freckles the dog, and Baby. In my opinion, the most important item was Baby. It held the liquor. Obviously, I was now with the Catholics, not the Methodists.

When we reached our hotel around midnight, someone handed me Freckles's leash and said to go walk the dog. If I hadn't known my place before, I knew it now. When I finally entered the hotel, I walked down a red carpet where a crowd lined up several people deep waiting to see a Kennedy. Recognizing the dog, if not the person walking with him, someone called out to me, "Are you someone?"

Now how do you answer that kind of question? I was already a little deflated in my role as dog-walker, so my first reaction was to think, *No, I'm just the dog sitter.* Fortunately, I kept my mouth shut. It was then I looked around and realized *I* was on the red carpet, and at that moment, I was the only entertainment for these people who had probably been waiting hours to see a Kennedy. So with a little smile and a brighter attitude I kept walking and told myself, *I'm here now and I'm going to enjoy every minute of it.*

Now that I was officially on the traveling staff, Dick called me to his hotel room for a heart-to-heart talk. He cautioned that the lecherous reporters traveling with us would be hot on my trail if I gave them any encouragement at all. Therefore, I should be very careful because I could be certain that whatever I did and whomever I did it with would get around the press corps as fast as if it had been put out on the AP wire. That got my attention. When the little brotherly lecture ended and he walked me to the door, I took a closer look at him. I just hoped when we opened the door none of those gossipy reporters would be in the hall to see me leaving his room with him in his boxers and T-shirt!

Carol set me straight on the hierarchy of the traveling staff. Angie Novello was Robert Kennedy's private secretary. Fred Dutton, as the chief of staff, was the first person in the morning and the last person at night to see the candidate. The speechwriters, Adam Walinsky, Peter Edelman, and Jeff Greenfield, had been Bobby's aides and speechwriters in his office and now traveled with him. Dick Drayne, my boss in Ted Kennedy's office, was now Robert Kennedy's traveling press secretary. Lastly, there was Carol Welch, a young woman from RFK's Washington office and me, the candidate's traveling secretaries.

Angie, powerful and protective of her position, had in the past managed to eliminate other secretaries who had become too close to the candidate. One of her roles had been as his valet. And since Angie wouldn't like any one of us appearing to be too close to *her* senator, we decided, for safety's sake, that our role as valet would be performed in unison. We would be like a school of fish so Angie couldn't point to any individual and eliminate her.

Carol had worked in the Johnson White House with Bill Moyers when he was press secretary, and with her experience in traveling with the president, she became our natural leader. She insisted that we should be invisible, not only for our protection from Angie, but also because the exhausted candidate wouldn't want us in his way when he finally reached the peace and quiet of his room.

So we would unpack his bags as soon as we checked into our rooms. Since he usually worked the crowds or had meetings, we had time to do our thing before he came to his room. We laid out his grooming supplies and his clothes for the next day, including underwear, then laid out his pajamas and pulled back the bed covers. Sounds simple, doesn't it?

Well, not so fast. Whoever packed his things at his home, Hickory Hill, must have thrown every toilet article he ever owned into his kit. There were several brands of toothpaste, multiple kinds of razors and shaving creams, a sleeping mask, foundation makeup (for his wife, Ethel? Or for him to apply before TV interviews?), and assorted other things one might need sometimes, but not on every trip. And which did he prefer, the electric razor, the single-edge, or double-edge razor? Which kind of cream? So we usually put everything out for him to choose for himself.

Then there were his suits, blue shirts and white shirts, ties, socks, underwear, and so on. The sight of three single young women racing around the room deciding what a presidential candidate should wear is not pretty. In a hurry, we would each grab something: a suit, a shirt, a tie, and then come together, look at them, and say, "Well, maybe this would do better," and exchange something. We had no clue what his preferences were. We'd carefully lay out his undershorts, T-shirt, and socks. On the bed would be his PJs. Did he really need the sleeping mask? His suit, shirt, and tie were on a chair. We were careful not to disturb many of his things so we could quickly pack up in the morning. And then we were out of there.

Because we had our own stuff to pack and we were always short of time, only one of us would pack his bags in the morning. We'd laid everything out in the evening, so it was beyond us why he sometimes had to paw through the neatly packed suitcases for fresh underwear that was exactly like what we'd laid out for him. It must be a man thing. And he wasn't always wearing the suits or shirts we'd selected. Bottom line? It took the packer a lot of time to get out of there in the morning.

When we arrived at the plane, we'd check with each other to find out how bad it had been that morning. Our shorthand question was, "Is he wearing our shorts?" If he wasn't, then the room had been a disaster and the packer had had her hands full repacking everything. Eventually the press picked up on this and as they filed onto the plane, they'd ask the same question: "Is he wearing your shorts today?"

One day a young local reporter who had joined us for a couple of legs of our trip overheard the battle-hardened national reporters asking this important question, and he leaped into action. With his notepad and pencil at the ready, he turned to us girls asking why that was important. While we floundered for an answer, he then quickly turned to someone else to ask the same question. Obviously, he felt he was on to something. As I looked on hopelessly trying to come up with an explanation that wouldn't be horrifyingly embarrassing to read in the newspaper, a senior reporter took the cub reporter by the shoulder and walked him to his seat, whispering in his ear. That seemed to answer his question because he quickly put his notebook away and grabbed a drink.

No matter how early we boarded the plane, after determining the answer to the all-important question of the candidate's underwear selection, the next question from us was, "Can I have a Bloody Mary?" It became so routine, the stewardesses eventually delivered them without being asked.

We did such a great job of being invisible that one day as we were standing at the curb watching a high school band play and cheerleaders jump around singing the campaign song and waving their pom-poms,

Bobby emerged from the hotel, once again not wearing what we'd laid out for him. Spotting us, he walked over, parted the crowd, and called out to us, "Girls, it's a blue shirt for day and a white shirt for night."

Obviously, the care and grooming of a presidential candidate was being done on the run. While we were carefully playing the invisible staff to afford him a semblance of privacy, there were times when that wasn't an option. Robert Kennedy had a mop of hair that hung over his forehead curling upward when it got long. He seemed to constantly push it away from his face. His caricatures in newspapers depicted him with big front teeth and that hair. People who didn't like him usually pointed to it and declared they wished they had a pair of scissors so they could cut that thing off.

I was in Fred's room one day helping him with some letters when Robert Kennedy walked in and immediately flopped facedown onto the sofa. What I saw was a back, and without thinking twice I rose to give him a back massage. But even before I could walk across the room, the exhausted candidate was sound asleep. After a short nap a barber arrived to give the senator a haircut. As he finished the trim, RFK looked in the mirror and suggested he shorten the hank of hair some more. And then with a twinkle in his eye he quipped he had thought the barber would have been eager to cut it shorter. And the barber, who had had the opportunity so many people longed for, grimaced as he trimmed it further and confessed that he hadn't wanted to cut his trademark too short.

While there were certain reporters permanently assigned by their organizations to travel with each candidate's campaign, there were others who moved back and forth between the two. We always sought out those people to hear how Eugene McCarthy's campaign was doing. How were the crowds, really? What were their impressions of the other guy? Was their campaign well organized? What kind of energy did McCarthy generate in his organization, in the crowds? We were hungry for information because, surrounded by the press as we were, we seldom had time to read the papers or to watch television news shows. (Remember we didn't have news shows running twenty-four hours a day.) It was like Samuel Taylor Coleridge's poem, "The Rime of the Ancient Mariner": "Water, water, everywhere/Nor any drop to drink."

We were often surprised by the answers to our questions. How McCarthy would apparently skip a stop from apparent lack of interest or perhaps too small a crowd. There was an absence of energy and excitement on the trail as compared to our campaign. The dedication of the young people knocking on doors and rallying around him evoked envy and wonder in us that they had not abandoned him for our man, who we felt was so worthy of their support. After all if their candidate wasn't willing to put in the effort, why was he still out there? McCarthy just wouldn't go away.

A Side Trip

Ohio looked iffy for Kennedy, and with the caucuses coming up, he needed to make a big impression on the delegates to encourage as many of them as possible to either stay uncommitted or to come over to him. So he made a quick trip to Columbus, Ohio, and for some reason I can't recall, it was decided (probably by Carol) that I should go alone and take care of the senator that night. We would return the next day and pick up everyone left behind.

The advance men had done a superb job of turning out a huge crowd in Columbus. People lined the highway from the airport to downtown. The candidate rode in a convertible, standing either on the backseat or on the trunk, with Rosey or Rafer holding on to keep him from being pulled from the car. As usual, the press rode directly behind him in a big bus; I rode in a Cadillac with the baggage at the end of the procession. The campaign avoided putting the candidate in an expensive car in a caravan, preferring an open convertible for better visibility. In this case, the volunteer had obviously brought his father's car with the hope of maybe driving the candidate—instead he got me. He didn't seem happy.

The image of the whole campaign that stays strongest in my mind is that trip into town and the crowds that greeted him. People had come out to see a Kennedy, but seeing wasn't enough. They needed to touch him. There was such a press of people surrounding the car that it could only travel at a snail's pace. His cuff links, which we must have bought by the gross, were quickly stripped from him. He then rolled his sleeves up to his elbows and reached out to touch as many people as he could. I have a photo of him silhouetted against the sun, surrounded by arms reaching up to the sky to find him. It's a picture you won't see today because the Secret Service would insist on much more crowd control than was evident that day.

It was taking so long to travel the route that eventually my car peeled out of line and headed to the hotel so I could get the rooms set up before the candidate arrived. I had plenty of time. A trip that normally took twenty minutes took two hours that day. I watched from the candidate's room as he came into view, looking like a Pied Piper pulling everyone along with him. The street below the hotel was a mass of people surging toward him.

When he eventually arrived at the room, everyone was jubilant. "That should send a message to the uncommitteds," someone said. And it must have, because we succeeded in preventing McCarthy from winning the state. Instead, the Ohio delegation would be up for grabs at the convention, where we certainly expected to carry the day.

The next morning, I ordered room service, drew a hot tub, and woke the senator. I'm sure he needed a long hot soak to ease the aches and pains from the battering he had received the night before at the hands of the crowd. Later when we left the hotel, the borrowed car the campaign had used for the senator's triumphant entrance into town was parked by the front door. It was amazing. The car was crushed. There was not a panel on it that was not significantly dented from the bodies being pressed against it. To me it looked totaled.

From Columbus we were on to Portland, Oregon. By now it was obvious that I was on the campaign, at least through the western swing. Why, you may ask, was I so important to the campaign? Well, my theory is that (1) everyone liked the easy access to the candidate without Angie there to guard the door, and (2) I gave good back massages.

At two o'clock in the morning when one is trying to stay awake and write something meaningful, it's helpful to have a nice relaxing massage, and I was the expert. We existed on about four hours of sleep a night. Each speech, once it was finalized, had to be typed on a stencil and then run off on the hand-cranked mimeograph machine, collated, and stapled. Meanwhile, the speech copy was typed on the large font typewriter and put into a notebook for the candidate. And a copy of the speech had to be faxed to the Washington, DC, office. The difficulty came from the lateness of the final approval of the speech since the senator usually didn't see it until he dragged himself back to his room after the evening's rally and meetings with the locals. Often, we typed the revised versions on the plane with the typewriters in our laps; we rarely used the Selectrics because the way they were fixed to the tables made it awkward for us to reach them.

When I had packed for this leg of the campaign, I expected to be gone a week. Now that I'd made the cut, I needed more clothes. So I took a couple of hours to go shopping in two nice department stores in Portland. I found a cute little striped sleeveless minidress that I ended up wearing constantly, it was so comfortable. (After the campaign, when I was back in DC at my apartment building's swimming pool, I discovered to my horror that my adorable minidress was really a swimsuit cover-up! Oops!)

As I stood on the street corner juggling my packages, I discovered I had shoplifted a tote bag. There among my numerous packages was a tote I couldn't remember ever seeing. Any minute I expected a cop to collar me. All I could think of was the headline, Kennedy Staffer Caught Shoplifting! I scurried back to the last store I'd been in, slipped through the doors, and raced to the counter at which I had made my last purchase. I was a nervous wreck as I showed the clerk the tote and told her what I'd done. She couldn't have cared less.

A Fateful Strategy Session

It quickly became obvious that Kennedy was going to lose Oregon, so I didn't stay there long. Instead, I was assigned to the Los Angeles office for the remainder of the Oregon campaign. However, there was one fateful meeting I did attend before moving on to Los Angeles.

We had taken a quick trip to San Francisco in order for RFK to make a speech. While he was doing his thing, Peter Edelman, Jeff Greenfield, Adam Walinsky, Milton Gwertzman, Carol, and I had dinner at the Fairmont Hotel and discussed the importance of winning California, particularly in light of our impending loss in Oregon. Kennedy's top advisors hashed over numerous scenarios for the California campaign: how to get free media coverage in such a huge state, whether to have a debate with McCarthy, what were the significant voter blocks, and how to get them on board.

There was a large block of Jewish voters in California and the advisors decided it would be the smart thing for the candidate to promise, if elected, to sell Israel the F-14 fighter planes they had long been asking for. This was a very big deal. Jeff, who would soon be taking a few days off to get married, would write the speech just as soon as he returned from his wedding. The candidate could give it at a prominent synagogue where he was already booked to speak. It would create a great deal of publicity and it would certainly appeal to the Jewish vote.

As expected, we did indeed lose Oregon. It was going to be close in California so all the troops were called in. Ethel, RFK's wife, and the six youngest children arrived to appear with him. Ted Kennedy worked the San Francisco and Northern California area, John Glenn, America's first man in space, and his wife went where needed, John Stewart of the Kingston Trio traveled with us and sang, and there was a big, glamorous fundraising gala attended by tons of celebrities. JFK's advisors joined us and of course all the national press came for the countdown. It was a pressure cooker.

Dick Drayne and Adam Walinsky reviewing the press statement after the Oregon loss.

Jeff returned to the campaign with his bride and joined us at the Ambassador Hotel. Time was running out and the speech wasn't ready—not a new thing, but it was frustrating. The senator was to give the speech the next evening and hadn't signed off on it yet. Jeff promised to work on it after dinner. Next it was 11 p.m. Finally, he told me to go to bed; he'd wake me at six o'clock, and we'd finish it then. Obviously Jeff was distracted.

We worked on it that morning, but there just wasn't enough time. He needed to get it to the senator at eight o'clock, before he left on a long motorcade that was heading to the southern part of the state. We watched the clock; Jeff composed, I typed, and we checked the time again and again. Then we remembered, Ethel would be with him and that meant the motorcade couldn't possibly start on time because she was always late. Jeff grabbed the draft of the speech and raced to the lobby. It was 8:20, but for once Ethel was on time. The motorcade was long gone.

Jeff and I looked at each other and tried to think. What to do? Back in our rooms with the rest of the staff we devised a plan. Jeff and I would rent a car and catch up with the caravan. Then Jeff would join the senator in his car and go over the speech while I followed in the rental car. As soon as we had draft approval, Jeff would call the girls at the hotel with the revisions, and then they would fly to San Diego to meet the candidate and press corps with the speech and a press release. This was, after all, *the* big speech.

It seemed to take an eternity to catch the candidate. Since we didn't know exactly where he was, we couldn't take any shortcuts, we needed to follow his itinerary. We knew we were closing in on him when we stopped at a hospital to check if Robert Kennedy had been there yet. A nurse still reeling from the encounter said with a little bit of disgust in her voice that one member of the entourage, probably Dick having another nicotine fit, had had the nerve to ask her where a cigarette machine might be. She had replied, "Don't you know this is a cancer hospital?" Oops!

When we finally caught up, Jeff and the senator sat in the back of a convertible as they drove down the highway reviewing the speech and making some changes. While RFK spoke at a luncheon meeting, Jeff phoned in the revisions. The girls raced to the airport, insisting that all of their equipment go topside so they could have quick access to things. They put the typewriters in their laps and typed the speech while they flew. Then with the mimeograph machine on the ticket counter at the charter plane terminal, they cranked out the copies, collated and stapled them, and then handed the finished press releases to the press as they exited the campaign plane.

Almost everyone was happy. Jeff and I were happy that our plan had come together so well, the girls were delirious to have even pulled it off, the candidate was happy with the speech, the press was happy to have their copy in time for deadline, and Jewish voters were happy that Israel would be getting the F-14s. Apparently, the only person who wasn't happy was Sirhan Sirhan, who heard about it from the extensive press coverage. He bought a gun.

Death was an unspoken subject on everyone's mind. It was the elephant in the living room, rearing its ugly head every so often. Sometimes the reminders of who and what was at risk were subtle; other times, dramatic.

For example, one beautiful California day not long after leaving the dreary Oregon days behind, one member of the national press corps was looking longingly out the bus window when he made his decision. He stood up and announced to those sitting near him, "My deadline is past for the day. I'm taking the rest of the day off and sitting by the pool." We turned to watch him as he stood to retrieve his belongings until one of the reporters sitting near him, whose deadline had also passed, said quietly, "You'd better not." That was enough to make him pause, rethink his decision, and with a sigh, sit down and remain with us until the day's itinerary was finished. Nothing more was said, but everyone understood—if anything happened to Robert Kennedy, he needed to be there.

Another time, the motorcade went through San Francisco's Chinatown with Ethel sitting on the backseat of a convertible while

RFK stood waving to the crowd. Then someone in the street set off a string of firecrackers. They sounded like shots. Ethel ducked, the senator flinched but remained standing, and the press poured off the bus to check out the scene. False alarm.

Even during casual times when Bobby was simply enjoying himself, the thoughts were not far from the minds of the reporters. With the youngest of the Kennedy brood with him in Los Angeles, a trip to Disneyland was inevitable. It was a day off from campaigning, but of course the press followed along, and if they were there, then I was there too.

Just like any other family, the kids tugged on their parents' hands to go here and there, asked for ice cream, stood in line for rides, and got tired and had to be carried. It seemed like a typical family outing except for the crowd of reporters tramping along behind them. Still, it was a relaxed, fun afternoon.

A reporter from a local TV station spotted an ideal photo op coming up and took his camera crew ahead to get them into position to record the senator as he and his family walked by a shooting arcade. Seeing what he was planning, one of the senior national reporters walked over to him, shook his head, and told him not to do it. And he didn't.

The hotels in which we stayed wisely put as many of us as possible together not just on the same floor but on the same hall. It helped us because late in the evening we often were running back and forth to each other's rooms for stuff. Sometimes we were in our bathrobes. But by the time the campaign was well underway, we were unconscious of our wardrobe.

So John Glenn in his pajamas didn't think anything about poking his head out the door of his room sometime after midnight shortly before the California primary and, catching me in the hallway, asking for my help. He was on the hotel phone trying to arrange for a charter plane to take him to North Dakota and needed to transfer the call. Could I help him? After all the trouble he had getting the right people, he certainly didn't want to lose the call.

"Sure," I said. "Be happy to help you." So he opened the door wider and I went in and sat on the unmade part of the bed where he had obviously been sleeping with his wife. She rolled over to make a little more room for me, I talked to the hotel operator, transferred the call, and left. Didn't think any more about it, until later.

Waiting for the Results

The night before the primary, we had a spontaneous little party in my room. As we were sitting back having a drink, some of the press, who had been with us from the beginning, came drifting in. They knew who looked after Baby, the liquor, and they were thirsty. It was a fun time as John Hart did his impression of Billy Graham and we sang some songs and reminisced about events on the campaign. There were plans for RFK to go to Poland after the California primary and before the convention. We expected to have huge crowds welcoming him. Who knew, maybe they would be as big as the reception had been for his brother, Jack, in Berlin. The hope was that it would have a positive impact on the undeclared convention delegates as well as the voters back home. With that scenario, the likelihood was we'd be breaking up, with some of the staff not traveling anymore and some of the press being reassigned, so this was like a little farewell gathering.

We had the next day off while the voters of California decided our fate, so several of us jumped into a car and headed for the beach. The Kennedy family was planning to relax at the seaside home of Joe Mankiewicz, Frank's brother. In spite of the vitamin B-12 shots he was getting, the senator had almost collapsed the night before while giving a speech, so he desperately needed some peace and quiet. We had to make a quick stop there to deliver some papers to him. When the secretary who had run in with the papers returned, her face was a brilliant red. What happened? She fell into the car laughing and confessed that when she couldn't find anyone in the house, the rest of the family not having arrived yet, she went searching for the candidate on the patio. She found him all right. He was sunbathing in the nude!

While we waited for the returns to come in that evening back at the Ambassador Hotel, someone described an event that happened that afternoon with Bobby and his son, David, that reminded me of one of our family stories:

Dad used to talk about the time we were all at the beach and he saw his son take off into the ocean, heading out to a sandbar. He had previously told Phil not to try it alone as the distance was too far for him. Now as he watched Phil, Dad could see he was going to try for it, so Dad dove in and took out after him. The waves breaking over the sandbar were so strong they kept pushing Phil back. He couldn't get a toehold and began to tire. Just as he turned to look for help, there was Dad to give him the extra push to safety. It was a story Dad told several times, I believe because it frightened him to think what could have happened if he hadn't been there.

And so it was with David. His father saw him swimming too far out in the ocean and, anticipating that his son might get into trouble, he dove in and took out after him. Sure enough, David had swum too far and as he began to flounder, his father reached him and helped him back to shore.

Later the press made a big deal out of RFK saving his son's life. But all I saw was a loving father who, despite the chaos of his own life, kept his eye on his children so he could be there to help when needed. Not a big deal; he simply did what all good fathers do: he watched over his children.

Counting the votes seemed to take forever, and as we waited in the candidate's suite, I went down to the ballroom on an errand. I couldn't enter, however, because I didn't have a ticket or the appropriate identification badge. Our security badges, a new thing, were to be handed out after the primary when we returned to DC. One of the national reporters saw me being turned away and asked if I was having trouble. When I said they wouldn't let me in, he chuckled and said to follow him. He took me through the press room to the kitchen and then on to the ballroom. He said it was the only way to do it as it was much too crowded to fight my way through the crowd to the far end of the ballroom where Pierre had a set up a mini command post, which was my destination. I used the route several times that evening.

As midnight neared, CBS finally projected Robert Kennedy as the winner in California. The late hour meant most of the country would miss his acceptance speech, so the senator quickly left for the ballroom. On his way out the door, he went to the secretaries sitting on the sofa watching the returns on TV and gave each a kiss on the cheek, and then he acknowledged the other people in the room, a number of whom were waiting to go to dinner with him, and left.

We watched his acceptance speech and when he said, "And now it's on to Chicago," and turned to leave, we lowered the volume on the TV and began chatting among ourselves. Almost immediately the phone rang; it was the direct line from the command post in the ballroom to the suite. I answered it, and Pierre said slowly and distinctly, "Something has happened to the candidate. Find out what it is. I'll wait."

Well, there certainly had not been enough time for Senator Kennedy to reach us, and as I checked among our group, they obviously knew nothing. I assumed he had fainted as he almost did a day or so before. But as I turned toward the TV, I could see something was happening, so I turned up the volume. Some stranger was at the microphone asking if there was a doctor in the house. And as difficult as it was to believe, a reporter said the senator had been shot in the head. Since I couldn't believe I had heard correctly that he, like his brother, had been shot in the head, I kept thinking the reporter was saying "the hip." It was incomprehensible.

A staff member leaned in the door and asked about the children. So I called the other hotel where they were staying with a babysitter, a young neighbor from McLean. He said the kids were all asleep except for David, who was watching everything on TV. It didn't seem to me there was much anyone could do for them at that point, and there was certainly no way David was going stop watching the television and go to bed now, so I said to stay with him; the sitter said he would, and I hung up. (It was David who subsequently died of a drug overdose alone in a Palm Beach hotel in the 1980s.)

The trouble was downstairs. Perhaps I could be of use. And since I thought the senator had been shot in the ballroom, I took my usual route through the kitchen. I found bedlam. What had previously been a well-ordered kitchen performing its routine tasks in a highly choreographed ballet of waiters, chefs, and busboys was now teeming with all the photographers, cameramen, journalists, and reporters who could fit into the room, as well as spectators, paramedics, and anyone else who could squeeze in. Everyone was jockeying for positions to see what was happening. Reporters and TV cameramen began shouting questions at me, wanting to know what I had seen, where I had been, and what I knew. I ignored them. I was busy looking for Dick.

The senator had already been removed to a hospital, but five other people had been shot and were on stretchers with EMTs working on them while they waited amid the chaos to be transferred to ambulances. It took only a couple of minutes to realize that Dick Drayne was not around, that he was probably at the hospital and there was really nothing useful I could do there, so I headed back to the candidate's suite.

People were milling around the lobby, some were kneeling at sofas in prayer while cameramen filmed them; others were weeping and wailing while reporters observed them and took notes. Everyone was shocked and no one really knew what, if anything, to do. So they just wandered around in stunned disbelief.

Back at the suite there was pandemonium. Those celebrities who had planned to go to a victory dinner with the candidate were still there weeping loudly and drinking a great deal. But we had things to do, so we gave them some liquor, closed them off from the main room of the suite, and settled in to handle the next phase.

The Kennedy family members who weren't there needed to be. Transportation had to be arranged, rooms found, updates given. Before long, I accepted the fact that the campaign was over and went to the staff's suite, which was directly below the senator's suite. I called home, waking Mother and Dad to tell them what had happened. We talked for a little while, and then I hung up and began packing our stuff.

At some point, someone brought a busboy to the suite to await the police, who wanted to talk to him. He was the young man with his hand under the senator's head in that photograph that became so widely shown. We couldn't talk; he didn't speak English, I didn't speak Spanish. But there really wasn't anything to say.

By morning, the word was out that all the campaign workers were to be packed and ready to leave California that day. There would be two charter planes heading east. One would go to Boston and New York, the other would go south to Washington, D.C. Be on one of them or pay your own way home later; the campaign needed to stop spending money immediately.

A Sad Trip Home

Kathleen, Joe, and Robert Kennedy Jr. were back east at school. President Johnson flew them by air force plane to Los Angeles to be with their parents, while the six younger children, along with John Glenn and his wife, would board the plane for the return trip home. The traveling campaign staff (i.e., us), decided we would return to Washington with the family. I think departure was around ten o'clock that morning, less than twelve hours after Robert Kennedy was shot.

As I packed first Dick's bag and then mine, a reporter, Sylvia Wright, and a photographer, Bill Eppridge, both from *Life* magazine stretched out on my bed, too emotionally spent to do anything but watch me work. Sylvia kept saying, "I can't believe how calm you are. You aren't crying or anything." That's because I was shell-shocked. But more importantly, I knew that first you handle the crisis. Later you can collapse.

At one point as I was standing in the hall, I ran into one of the national reporters who had been part of our entourage. He had been in the kitchen and somehow had found himself wedged on top of a refrigerator looking down at Ethel as she knelt beside her bleeding husband, surrounded by the bedlam in the kitchen. Looking up, she saw him watching her from his vantage point and, recognizing him, called to him, "Please, leave us alone."

With agony in his eyes, he told me he had not moved. Looking for redemption from me, he pled his case. "I'm a reporter; I couldn't leave."

Historical moments certainly require witnesses. We may vilify them at times, but society needs reporters. In the excitement of an unexpected, life-changing event, one hopes for a clear, objective witness. Today's reporter, if he is doing his job well, is our unbiased witness telling us clearly what happened so we can draw our own conclusions. Besides, wasn't this what each reporter on the bus feared would happen and had not wanted to miss?

There was a phone message from Suzanne White Leimann waiting for me.

She worked for Salisbury's *Daily Times* then, and I knew what she wanted. She was a childhood friend and I owed her. So I gave her my only interview about Robert Kennedy's shooting. It ran on the front page of the paper. When I saw the piece, I thought that when I finally came out of the closet about working for the Kennedys, I had certainly done it in a big way. (But Mother had been right about keeping my association with the Kennedys out of the paper. Later when I came home for a rest, Mother came to my room and very quietly said she wanted me to see something she had received in the mail after Suzanne's article had appeared in the paper. She pulled an envelope from her pocket and showed me an anonymous piece of hate mail about me and my association with the Kennedys. It had come from someone in town and had obviously frightened her. But for me it was just another example of the hatred some people have for the Kennedys.)

The air force plane we flew home in was divided into three sections. It had an open area with no seats near the front of the plane, a section of several rows of canvas chairs with no seat belts (which was okay since most of us had stopped using them on the campaign plane about halfway through the western swing), and a closed-off section with bunk beds where the children could stretch out and where the Glenns stayed. There were no windows on the plane; it seemed appropriate to keep the sunny outside world from intruding into our cocoon of grief.

We quickly abandoned the canvas chairs to sit cross-legged on the floor in a circle and drink. The air force steward apologized for not having any liquor to offer us. Not to worry. I still had Baby, which was all we needed.

Bill Eppridge's famous photo of RFK sprawled on the floor with blood running from his head and the busboy at his side had yet to be published. The only news we had were bulletins from the hospital saying he was gravely wounded but still alive, so we really had no idea how bad he was. We tried to convince ourselves that if he was alive there was still hope. I probably led the chorus with that thought.

That evening after reaching my apartment, which seemed so utterly empty and quiet, Dick called to say the senator was not going to make it; it was just a matter of time until his heart gave up. Dick said he was heading out that evening for New York to begin working on funeral arrangements. Once the senator's death occurred, which would probably be sometime that night, I should take the shuttle to New York to help him.

Late that evening, Frank Mankiewicz announced Robert Kennedy's death. He was forty-two years old.

A State Funeral

When the senator had announced his campaign for the presidency, the Kennedy Machine arrived on the doorstep to help with his race. Now a new cadre of people came out of the woodwork to help with his funeral. One person had the invitation lists from JFK's funeral, another knew how to set up the press at the church, someone else was knowledgeable about Arlington National Cemetery, and so it went.

In just a few short days we were able to put on a state funeral without the state's help.

Robert Kennedy lay in state at St. Patrick's Cathedral in New York City, and nearly a hundred thousand people, many with briefcases in hand, lined the streets for blocks and blocks, waiting patiently to walk by his casket. Friends, family, and members of his staff formed an honor guard that watched over him night and day until the funeral service. It was later estimated that five thousand people an hour walked past his flag-draped casket. So many people were touching the casket as they passed by that it began to rock. Someone commented later that he began to wonder if Bobby was going to rock right off the platform.

Dick and I stopped by the church and headed toward the side door. A TV reporter doing man-in-the-street interviews came up to us, thrusting his microphone into our faces, and asked, "And where were you when the senator was shot?" We shook our head to indicate we had nothing to say and walked on. When we were well beyond him, Dick turned and said, "I guess if we had told him where we were, we would have knocked his socks off."

The funeral service was by invitation only, and there was a wild scramble for them. Even though St. Patrick's is a large cathedral, seating was limited.

Many prominent people who felt they should be invited stood in line at our temporary funeral headquarters complaining over not having received their telegram of invitation.

Of course access was also limited for the press, and when the *New York Times*, which had never been particularly friendly to the Kennedys, asked for twenty-eight seats, there was a friendly argument among the various press secretaries as to who would have the privilege of telling them they could have only eight seats.

Ted Kennedy gave the eulogy and barely got through it. He ended with a quote from Robert Kennedy's stump speeches that his brother used almost every time he spoke. Once when he omitted the quote, some of the reporters objected because they had learned to rely on it as a signal that the end of his speech was approaching and that it was time to head to the buses. The quote from George Bernard Shaw came to characterize Robert Kennedy's campaign:

Some men see things as they are and say, "Why?"
I dream things that never were and say, "Why not?"

Buses lined the street beside the cathedral to take invited guests to a train that would carry Robert Kennedy to his final resting place. I grabbed a seat on one of them and watched as other guests, great and small, boarded. Milton Berle, or Uncle Miltie to millions of TV viewers, boarded my bus. By far his loud weeping surpassed everyone else's quiet mourning. It sounded so much like the sobbing I had heard that night back at the senator's suite in the room where his dinner guests were gathered that it made me wonder if he had been there too. In any case, the "spotlight" even on the bus was on him.

Ethel had never liked flying and chose to take a special train to Washington, DC, for interment. The casket, sitting high enough to be seen through the windows with the family gathered around it, was in the last car. Guests were in the middle cars having a fine wake, and the very subdued press and staff found their way to the forward cars where we sat in numb solitude, all of us in our own little worlds.

Although the train went relatively slowly, there were accidents along the way. Two people standing on the tracks were killed when a train coming from the opposite direction hit them. Another death occurred when someone standing on top of a train car on a siding slipped as we went by, grabbed an electrical wire, and was electrocuted. We knew what had happened because the networks were following the train on live TV. And with that, the train slowed to a crawl. A trip that normally took four hours ended up taking eight hours.

From New York City to Washington I don't think there was ever a hundred feet without someone standing beside the tracks watching him go by. It took hours to reach Baltimore, but still the people waited with signs, flags, and banners. It reminded me of the stories of President Lincoln's return to Illinois after his assassination. Adults and children stood at attention, hands over their hearts or holding flags and signs. And written across their faces was the same shock we were feeling. They were as heartbroken at what had happened to our country and to this family as we.

At some point in the long train ride, sixteen-year-old Joe, Robert Kennedy's oldest son, walked the length of the train thanking supporters, staff, and press alike for being there, listening in turn to their words of sympathy and, in many cases, promises of support in the future. We in the press car observed that the next generation was already stepping forward, learning the trade. Then Ethel made the long walk through the train, thanking everyone for being there.

Ralph Abernathy, who had assumed leadership of Martin Luther King Jr.'s long-planned Poor People's Campaign, took the opportunity to walk the length of the train, too, seeking support for the poor people he had left behind in DC camping in tents and shacks in the mud of the National Mall. They were there in an effort to bring the nation's attention to the plight of the poor. While everyone else wore suits to the funeral, he wore overalls so no one could miss the message. We in the press car thought he would have been more effective if he had not been wearing his expensive, well-polished, wing-tipped shoes.

In Baltimore the train stopped for a choir to sing "Battle Hymn of the Republic," which had been sung so beautifully by Andy Williams at the funeral mass. When we reached DC it was dark, so it must have been eight-thirty or nine o'clock. I joined the press in their bus. But in lining up the procession, someone had put the press bus near the rear of the motorcade. The press corps who had traveled with RFK on his campaign expressed a great deal of indignation at this slight and urged the driver to move forward to their usual location just behind the senator—which he did, putting us in front of some mighty important people who ended up breathing our fumes.

The procession went by the Justice Department, where Robert Kennedy had served as attorney general for his brother, and then we paused in front of the Lincoln Memorial for another performance of "Battle Hymn of the Republic." Finally, we arrived at Arlington.

The interment was by candlelight. There were hundreds, maybe thousands, of people there awaiting the senator's arrival. His older sons and close friends and some staff were the pallbearers. Fortunately, there were more than six of them because as they began the uphill climb with the heavy casket, the TV lights came on and blinded them; disoriented, they became just a little bit lost. It became a long hike. Eventually they began muttering among themselves, "Bobby is probably wondering if we're ever going to get him there," . . . "Yeah, who advanced this trip?" . . . "Are you sure we're going the right way?"

But it wasn't noticeable and after a small U-turn, they did eventually reach the grave site where we sang yet another round of the "Battle Hymn of the Republic" and then laid him to rest near his brother, Jack.

Only eighty-five days had passed from the beginning of the campaign to its end, from the day he announced to the day he was buried.

Robert F. Kennedy in Retrospect

People have asked me my impressions of Robert Kennedy. He seemed at times to be almost shy, and at other times his presence was electrifying. If he and his brother, Ted, were at the same party, Ted would have been leading the singing of Irish songs and being generally a hail-fellow-well-met, while Bobby would probably have been standing in a corner with a couple of aides discussing some issue.

What is there about witnessing something that really is inconsequential in and of itself, but future events remind you of it and lock it into your mind forever?

Robert Kennedy was a gentleman who, in the rough and tumble campaign atmosphere, would instinctively clean up his act in front of a woman. Just prior to the California primary, he stormed into Fred Dutton's room while I was typing some correspondence for Fred. RFK was obviously upset that John Glenn had chartered a jet, the one I had helped him with, so he could fly to a rally in North Dakota. "He could have... [pausing as he saw me there trying to be invisible, but with my rabbit ears up to catch every word, he changed the expletive he so obviously intended to use] . . . *bloody well* gone commercial many times over for what that flight cost." Fred mollified him by pointing out that Glenn had wanted to be back in California in time to be with him when the returns came in for that important primary.

At a time when race relations were extremely sensitive (even Salisbury had race riots during the campaign), he seemed to be the one person who could bring differing factions together. Frequently during campaign stops when he was touching the people who had come out to see him, he would be grasping a black hand with one hand and a white one with his other hand. The eager expressions on both people's faces showed their trust that he would be the conduit for a peaceful reconciliation between races. It seemed to epitomize his campaign: blacks and white reaching out, with him as the intermediary.

Interestingly enough, television interviews really did not help him much in his quest for office because he was so stiff and uncomfortable. However, people in cities and towns across America would pour out of their houses and shops to see him drive by. If he came to their area, they would come to see the celebrity but stay to hear the politician and then vote for him. If he didn't personally go to an area, he probably didn't carry it.

For me Hickory Hill symbolizes the Kennedys. If Jack Kennedy's administration had been Camelot, its headquarters had been Bobby and Ethel's home at Hickory Hill. The house, shaded by big old trees, sits on nearly six acres. It is a wonderful white brick home with a labyrinth of rooms, a tennis court, swimming pool, and pool house, and plenty of yard for the touch football games.

President Kennedy's campaign in the '60s had been to bring new vigor to the White House, and the rough and tumble spirit of the Kennedys had been epitomized with their touch football games on the grounds at Hickory Hill. Here the powers-that-be or wanted-to-be met and talked and played. Here they tossed guests at formal parties into the swimming pool; here they hammered out domestic policies on the tennis court or conducted quiet diplomacy under the huge oak trees.

And here I was, invited to Hickory Hill.

Ethel had always attended Mass every day, and after her husband's death she gathered her family, friends, and those who had worked with him (including me) around her. So on several occasions I found myself attending Mass at their little church in McLean followed by brunch at Hickory Hill.

Eventually Ethel, who was three months pregnant with her eleventh child when RFK died, moved to their Cape Cod home for the summer. There she could be near her extended family as well as her support group of friends. She generously offered Hickory Hill as a summer retreat for the office and campaign staffs, and we took full advantage of it.

There was very little work to be done at either senator's office. Robert Kennedy's office was, of course, closing down, sorting out materials, and getting ready for the new occupant. I returned to work at Ted Kennedy's office, but it was also low-key because the senator was so deeply in mourning for his brother that he never came in. He, too, spent the summer at the Cape.

We used Hickory Hill like a private club and while the house was not open to us, the pool house was. We lounged at the pool, played tennis and football, and got to know each other a little better. One of those people was Mary Jo Kopechne, who I already knew on a limited basis through her roommate, Nance Lyons, who worked in my office. While she was not exactly shy, Mary Jo was a quiet person who was likely to fade into the background at a party. She had worked in Robert Kennedy's office before the campaign.

This being a Kennedy home, a contest of some sort was usually involved in the play. One evening we had a relay race in the pool and, naturally, everyone was required to participate. Mary Jo didn't want to compete, saying she just wasn't a good enough swimmer to be on anyone's team. We all insisted, and she finally ended up on my team.

She was correct, she was a poor swimmer. Mary Jo was obviously very ill at ease in the water. She continually bumped into the wall, never lifted her head from the water, and became very much disoriented. However, with a lot of hollering and coaxing from the sidelines, she finally reached the end. I think that, even as determined as she was, without our encouragement she would have called it quits shortly into her leg of the relay. At the time I only cared that we had lost the race. Later I would recall how very uncomfortable she had been in the water.

I had a couple of dates with an advance man from the campaign who was house-sitting for Ethel. It was really nice to be able to poke around the house a little without offending anyone. Perhaps here I would find some explanation for what motivated a person to bet his life that he could make a difference in American politics.

Hickory Hill was a home steeped in history. Everywhere one looked, there were powerful historical memorabilia—only here, the photos were personal family shots. I saw many framed snapshots of Jackie Kennedy and Ethel, sometimes with a little funny note attached to the frame, or of President Kennedy just being one of the guys. There were candid photos of famous American and international politicians, military leaders, and others who were household names to Americans, but for the Kennedys, they were simply family friends or family members.

Displayed on a large easel in the entrance hallway was one of three original handwritten copies of the Emancipation Proclamation, signed by Abraham Lincoln. Robert Kennedy's reading material was in bookcases, in easy reach of his chair. Here were bookmarked and dog-eared books written by the great philosophers of the ages, such as Voltaire, Locke, Camus, and others obviously well and repeatedly read, for there were handwritten notations in the margins. Those shelves were the heart of Robert Kennedy's intellectual searching. What a privilege it was to sit and read the comments he had jotted in the margins on page after page of those books.

If you want to achieve a goal, motivational speakers will advise you to hang pictures of your goals on the walls or write and read positive affirmations attesting to that toward which you strive. Robert Kennedy did that. He surrounded himself with greatness—great men, great minds, great actions. After seeing his personal sanctuary, it seemed to me inevitable that he would want to strive for greatness himself. That he would want to try to change his dreams into reality. That he would believe one person *could* make a difference.

Having rummaged—a little—through the Kennedys' lives at Hickory Hill, talked to their friends at the brunches, and seen and felt the joy and despair they experienced, I learned an important lesson during my years working in Washington. It was that no matter how important a person is, ultimately, we all have the same interests and concerns as the next person—even though that person may play a role on a larger stage.

While our lives—at least those of us associated with the Kennedys—seemed to be on hold, the rest of the world kept moving forward. Or, as Robert Frost once observed, "In three words I can sum up everything I've learned about life. It goes on."

The Torch Is Picked Up

The Democratic Convention was to be held in August and the race between Vice President Hubert Humphrey and Senator Eugene McCarthy was coming down to the wire; a lot of people, particularly Kennedy supporters, weren't happy about either candidate. A ground swell of enthusiasm developed toward drafting Ted Kennedy for president.

He didn't want any part of it, but the senator did agree to give a foreign policy speech prior to the convention. The night before the speech was to be given in Worcester, Massachusetts, Dick Drayne and I were at the senator's house in Georgetown working on yet another draft. The tension was reminiscent of the aborted presidential campaign.

To add to the tension, the Kennedys had been invited to an after-concert dinner that night at the Mellons' (of banking fame) home and were running late. As he and his wife, Joan, walked out the door, the senator was saying to her, just as any other husband would, "Do you know where we're going?"

She replied, "I have the address, but I'm not sure just where it is."

"Well, we'll just have to stop at a gas station and get directions," he said as he shut the door.

They sounded just like my brother and sister-in-law, already late and not knowing where they were going!

But that was fine. At least they were out of the house. Now, while Dick polished the speech, I had the house to myself to explore. It was stylishly decorated of course, but not as dramatically as their new home in McLean would be. As expected, the decor was heavy on photos and memorabilia. Pretending I was looking for a powder room, I even tiptoed upstairs, albeit somewhat guiltily, to poke around a little.

When he and his wife returned, the senator reviewed the rewritten speech with Dick while Joan and I talked. I admired Joan Kennedy and wished I could emulate her way of being totally focused on what a person was saying. When you were talking to her, her eyes never wandered off to check the room; they were locked on you. It was as if what you were saying was too important for her be distracted. I was always complimented by her attention.

This time it was I who was totally absorbed in what she was saying. Joan was wide-eyed with the wonder of having dinner with the Mellons. It had been a small, spectacular dinner party for twelve. The table was beautifully set with vermillion place settings, gorgeous crystal, and even a footman standing behind each guest. It was obviously beyond anything she had experienced; she wanted to talk about it to someone, and there I was.

Then with a guilty little laugh she confided that she really just had to poke around the house a little, so she did what most women have always done— asked to use the upstairs bathroom. As she was recounting her experiences, I couldn't help reflecting that we were certainly sisters-under-the-skin, for while she was exploring the Mellons' house, I had been exploring hers!

We entered a new ball game with the senator's foreign policy speech in Worcester. The world that listened so intently, first to Jack Kennedy's words, then to Robert Kennedy's words, now turned its attention to the last remaining brother, Ted Kennedy. Where before the senator's speeches had received minimum mention, even in the Massachusetts papers, now the world press wanted to know what he would say. His speech was carried live on all three networks, preempting the daytime soaps, of all things. He had really come a long way!

I had barely gotten the speech copy typed for him to take to Worcester, so there was no time to type the stencils and copy, collate, and staple the press releases before he left that morning. Therefore, while Dick and I flew to Worcester in the morning, I was typing the speech onto a stencil with the typewriter on my lap while he proofread the copy. A policeman met us at the plane and drove us with the siren screaming to the campus where the luncheon meeting and speech were to take place.

While Dick went to handle the press, I hurried to find a mimeograph machine and run off copies of the speech. Once collated, I grabbed the press copies and started running to the hall where the senator had already begun his speech. As I raced to the building, I heard the *click click* of rifles being cocked. I stopped and looked up—there on the rooftops of the buildings were sharpshooters pointing guns at me! That certainly got my attention. After identifying myself, a police officer ordered me to walk, not run, to the building, and you can believe I did exactly as he instructed.

The world had indeed turned. And while the senator was saying the torch had been passed to another brother, I found that from that day forward I would stand in the back of any hall where he was speaking and scan the audience, watching for someone to reach into a pocket and pull out a gun. I was fully prepared to jump on anyone who might threaten my senator.

CHAPTER FOUR

OVERCOMING TRAGEDIES

We thought, because we had power, we had wisdom.
—Stephen Vincent Benet

America was being torn apart. On one side of a great divide were young people and those who opposed the Vietnam War. On the other side was a stunned population who could not believe so many people could defy their government so loudly and violently. Within three months we had lost two national leaders through assassination, cities had burned, and tempers were boiling.

The Democratic Party had its convention in Chicago. With Gene McCarthy's young supporters agitating for a forum in which to express their feelings about the war, the tension was enormous. We watched on TV as the anger built both on the floor of the convention and in the streets, where the police and the youths confronted each other hourly. Gene McCarthy never went out to his supporters to try to defuse the tension, which we were confident Robert Kennedy would have done.

With so much pressure both inside and outside the hall, the convention definitely did not need Dick Tuck there fomenting more

Overcoming Tragedies

chaos. Dick was kind of short, with twinkling eyes and bushy hair. He looked like an Irish leprechaun. He had long been a lighthearted trickster for his Democratic candidates. At least if he were on your side, you tended to think of his antics as lighthearted and funny. I had never been quite sure what his role had been in our campaign, but at the convention he was definitely freelancing. Ultimately, he demonstrated that one person *can* make a difference, only with Dick there were many far-reaching, unintended consequences.

When Nixon toured Chinatown in San Francisco during John Kennedy's campaign, Dick arranged for a banner to stretch across a famous intersection with the words, "Chinatown Welcomes Vice President Nixon." (It was the same intersection where the firecrackers exploded in Bobby's campaign.) It made for a wonderful photo op and Nixon took full advantage of the opportunity. What he couldn't read was the Chinese message written under the English that said, "What about the Hughes deal?"—which was an embarrassing campaign issue for him. Another time, during the Johnson vs. Goldwater campaign, Dick Tuck arranged for the bleachers at a huge Goldwater rally to be painted just before the crowds arrived.

At this convention in 1968, Dick had printed up bogus floor credentials, handing them out to anyone who wanted them—and everyone wanted them. He packed the floor with McCarthy supporters. Pandemonium escalated into riots, people were injured, and the nation was shocked and horrified at the Democrats, who appeared to be completely out of control. Hubert Humphrey won the nomination but started his campaign in such a deep hole that there was not enough time for him to recover and win the election. Nixon won the presidency by a very narrow margin, but win he did.

After the campaign, the press office, which consisted of just Dick Drayne and me was moved to the main office where our tiny cubbyhole was squeezed into room number one. And what had been our office around the corner was taken over entirely by the senator's mail room.

I'm not sure exactly when I went to our former office around the corner from the main office to see what was going on there. It was now a hive of activity. There seven or eight volunteers opened and sorted the tremendous volume of letters we received, stuffing them into cubbyholes that lined both walls and marched down the center of the room.

Standing near the center row of mail sorters and chatting with one as she opened the mail, I noticed a mimeographed letter on a stack of letters at her station. For some reason unknown to me I did something I never did before or after that day.

As I leaned over and looked at a letter, I said to the volunteer "This is mimeographed and is obviously going to a lot of other senators. It should be his own senator's letter to reply to."

Then I picked up the letter and dropped it into the trash can. The volunteer said, "That letter came certified mail." I said something dismissing, I'm sure, turned and left the room.

Now it was our senator's office where the phones jangled off the hook, people rushed in and out, tourists loitered with hopes of shaking the senator's hand, people with appointments stood and waited, photographers and the press poked their heads in just to check on things, and aides walked and talked with people as they rushed to appointments.

People like to rationalize about not writing to their elected officials, saying that politicians don't care what the public thinks. Well, in our office we did keep track of the volume of mail on issues. Long before Nixon went to China, the senator gave a daring address, I think at the

United Nations, advocating opening trade between the United States and communist China. It was not a popular position. It generated a ton of mail.

At about the same time, the senator and his wife, Joan, attended a function at the White House. She looked lovely in a glittery silver cocktail dress. Well, it *was* rather short, but I thought she carried it off very well. However, there were a lot of people who didn't agree with me. One day I walked into a room to find the senator shaking his head in amazement at two tall stacks of letters. In one stack were the unfavorable letters about his speech. The other contained the unfavorable letters about the length of his wife's dress. Incredibly, more people were upset about Joan's minidress than about his advocacy for trade with China!

The senator and we were working harder than ever. It seemed that my hours increased from 9:00 a.m. to 6:00 p.m. to 9:00 a.m. until… I worked so many nights until 2:00 a.m. that if I'd leave by 11:00 p.m., friends in the office the next day would smile for me, pleased I hadn't had to work too late. Occasionally the sun was coming up as I headed for home. I loved it.

One time Dick and I were working late on a speech that we were to put under the senator's doormat at his home when finished so he could review it first thing in the morning. We badly underestimated the senator. Well, it was well after midnight, closer to one o'clock, and we sat staring at each other in a bit of a stupor. Dick said (very convincingly, I thought), "He'll never get up early to read the speech. He's at so-and-so's party, and you know he won't get home before two o'clock. I'll give it to him tomorrow morning when he comes in. That should be plenty of time."

It sounded reasonable to me until Dick told me the next day that he had been awakened at six o'clock by a call from the senator asking for the speech. Dick, who had expected to give it to him at nine o'clock at the very earliest, had to get up, get dressed, and have it on the senator's desk "no later than eight o'clock." We had known the senator didn't ask more of his staff than he did of himself, so we should have known better than to assume he couldn't rally in the morning. We never made that mistake again!

The Military and the Kennedys: No Love Lost

One of the senator's strengths with his constituents was his attention to their needs. Hence one person was assigned to handle the immigration case work, which was my job when I first began working for the senator. One person worked with mayors, helping them with grants and other issues affecting their communities. Another person was assigned to help members of the military and their families with issues they might have with their branch of the service. It seemed to me that many of those issues involved helping a service person get compassionate leave to go home for an emergency or a veteran to get his benefits. So it wasn't unusual to have someone in uniform sitting in the reception area waiting to meet with the caseworker.

At the height of the Vietnam War, I arrived one morning with my arms full of newspapers and saw a number of soldiers standing in the front office. Thinking they were there for the caseworker and, being me, I had to make some comment at having five or six soldiers there all at once. So I said with a smile, "Looks like the brass is out in full force today."

They turned toward me in unison. No responding smiles from them. Absolutely no sense of humor here. Quickly I checked their collars and saw a maple leaf and then one with a bunch of stars. *Uh-oh*. I kept on walking through the strained silence. When I reached my desk, I whispered to Dick what had happened. He rolled his eyes, grimaced a bit, and said, "Oh, that's General Westmoreland. He's here to see the senator." *Oops!*

As I learned over the years, the military didn't have a great deal of fondness for the Kennedys. Shortly after Robert Kennedy's death, a friend fixed me up with a blind date who was an air force pilot. It was so soon after the senator's death that the air was still crackling with the residual excitement of such a historical event. We were barely out of sight of my apartment building, driving to his base for dinner at the officers' club, when he said words to this effect (I can't remember them verbatim because they hurt so much, I put them out of my mind.)

"I'm sick and tired of all this talk about Kennedy's death. Frankly, I'm glad he's dead."

I turned to him and asked, "You do know I worked for Robert Kennedy and was with him in California when he was shot, don't you?"

"Yeah, I just want to set the record straight about where I stand on the Kennedys." And then he went on for about five or six minutes, making sure I understood how he felt.

Well, that was a fun date.

Another time I had a dinner date with a naval officer. His commanding officer had required his presence at an unscheduled dinner with him the night of our first date, which made him late for his dinner with me. That helped to set up an uncomfortable situation that I didn't do anything to relieve. We had such a bad time together that when we reached my door, we turned, looked at each other and agreed that "this was so awful maybe we should try it again. It's got to be better next time." So we did.

This time when he picked me up, he said his commanding officer had invited him to his house for drinks, and he had to go. Would I *please* not say *anything* about working for the Kennedys! Obviously, he was concerned about such a disclosure, so I promised to keep my mouth shut about them.

Well, we sat on the porch and chatted with his commanding officer, his wife, and teenage daughter. After a while, the wife, as any good naval officer's spouse has probably learned, turned to little ole silent me and inquired, "Do you work?"

"Yes, I do," I replied.

"Oh, where do you work?"

"In Washington."

"And where do you work in Washington?" she persisted, drilling down for a more complete answer.

Well, a promise is a promise, and I tried to keep mine. "Oh, I just work on the Hill," I replied.

She was tenacious. "Do you work in the Senate or the House?"

I looked at my date. He was glaring at me. Well, no help from that quarter; we could both see where this was going.

"The Senate," I said, casting a quick glance at her husband, who had leaned forward and put his elbows on his knees to apparently get a better look at me.

The inquisition continued.

"Who do you work for?" came the inevitable question.

With a quick, apologetic look at my date, I said, "Senator Kennedy."

Well, the wife and teenage daughter were ecstatic. They began bombarding me with questions: "What's he like? Is he as handsome in person as in pictures? Have you met his wife? What's it like working for someone so famous?" And on it went for a half hour or forty-five minutes. The two men never said a word... and I never heard from my date again.

Let's face it: my dating life at that point was not doing really well. I had recently broken up with Len, whom I had dated for a number of months. He was a sales representative for the Sands Hotel in Las Vegas. Once when he had a charter plane of high rollers to accompany to Vegas, he invited me to join him. We sat over the wing of the turboprop plane. It was early evening and still light when somewhere over the Midwest, the pilot announced in his smooth, no-need-to-panic voice that he was "having a little trouble with an engine," so he had taken the precaution of shutting it down. We would be making an emergency landing as soon as he found an airport.

It was the engine right outside my window where I could have an up-front and *very* close view of that still propeller. It was fascinating to be flying along with a propeller that wasn't moving. I turned to Len and said, "Can you see it okay?"

Apparently, he could. His face was white, his eyes were huge, and his hands had a viselike grip on the arm rests. *Dear me.* There was some damage control to handle next to me. So trying to reassure him, I pointed out there were three other engines working perfectly well, so we should be just fine. We landed safely and after about an hour, the problem was solved and we continued on.

Parents often have a good eye where dates are concerned and mine were not particularly thrilled with Len. Of course, the more they objected, the more I dug in my heels. Finally, when I was visiting Phil and Jacquie in Baltimore, Jacquie told me Mother was reconciled to my marrying him. I heaved a big sigh of relief and said, "Good, now I can break up with him." Just that weekend, while I was sitting in his kitchen talking, I had said something that made him angry and he threw what was in his hand at the wall I was leaning against. Unfortunately, he was cutting a sandwich at the time with a butcher knife and it missed me by inches as it buried into the wall near my head.

Jackie Adds an O

Because of our late hours at the office and the Capitol Hill police's practice of relaxing their vigilance on parking spaces near the office building around 9:30 a.m., I seldom made an effort to arrive before 9:45. One afternoon in October, Dick pulled me aside and asked me very quietly if I could please come to work on time the next day. I flippantly replied, "Sure, if you will be here too."

He said he planned to be there by nine o'clock because tomorrow would be a heavy news day and we both needed to be on time. I asked him what was happening and he said he couldn't tell me; just be there. He could see he had hurt my feelings by not confiding in me, but he stayed mum.

The next morning as I was getting dressed, standing there with nothing on but a puzzled expression and pondering what could be so newsworthy, two things happened simultaneously.

First, there was a loud knock on my door. The door opened and a man's deep voice said, "Phone company. You left your keys in the door. I'll put them here on the floor," and then he shut the door and went away.

And just then I figured out what Dick wasn't talking about, and I was furious.

When I stormed into the office, he was standing at his desk bracing for a scene. I looked him in the eye and said, "Jackie Kennedy is getting married, isn't she?"

Sheepishly he admitted she would be marrying Aristotle Onassis, a Greek shipping magnate. He was sorry he couldn't tell me the previous night, but he had been sworn to secrecy. Only a very few people knew, and if the word had gotten out prematurely all hell would have broken loose. As it was, Maxine Cheshire was hinting about it in her column that day.

I tried to hide my angry tears because I did understand why he couldn't tell me, but even so, his lack of trust hurt. He asked how I had arrived at my conclusion, and I explained since we must be controlling the news, I figured it had to be something about the family. I'd eliminated deaths, campaign announcements, births, and marriage announcements already except for the only person in the family old enough to get married who wasn't already— which was Jackie. And not only that, but I had left my keys in the door all night, and while I stood there with nothing on as I tried to figure the whole thing out, the phone man had scared the devil out of me when he opened the door to return the keys.

Dick looked at me, gave me one of his smirky little smiles, and said, "That must be really discouraging."

"What's discouraging?" I snarled at him.

With his voice laced with false sympathy, he said, "After leaving your keys in the door all night, the best you could do was to have the telephone man return them to you!" Hell, he was right about that, too.

Sometime weeks later, Angelique, the senator's personal secretary, showed me a sheet of yellow legal paper with notes the senator had scribbled and doodled as he secretly traveled to Europe to meet with Onassis to negotiate the prenuptial agreement for Jackie. They included random words underscored, boxed in, or reworked over and over, as one does when puzzling over something; words such as *divorce, excommunication,* and *security.* Jackie had said she wanted to leave America because it had become too dangerous for Kennedys. And indeed it was.

Handling Threats

Along with the increased public interest in Ted Kennedy came an increase in the number of death threats he received. Twice a week the Secret Service stopped by to pick up a stack of threatening mail, their thinking being that if someone threatened a senator, he could also be a threat to the president. We kept our copies of those letters in alphabetical order by city of origin so if the senator was scheduled to go to that particular city, we could pull that folder and send what information we had about threats on his life to alert the local police.

William F. Buckley Jr., who was a conservative author and commentator as well as the founder of the *National Review* magazine, forwarded a threat to us he had received. It was a bull's-eye target on an 8½ " x 11" sheet of paper with the senator's head superimposed on it. The writer's comment was something like, "He's next." And Mr. Buckley's comment was something like, "I don't know how you endure this. I'm forwarding it to you because I'm sure your office must have a way to track this kind of stuff."

While those threats were handled in an almost routine fashion, there were others that stood out. Once I was putting some papers on the senator's desk when I spotted a small snapshot leaning against the lamp. Since I didn't recognize the person, I asked Angelique who it was. She replied, "We're working under an active threat right now. That's someone who has threatened the senator, and we know he got on a bus with a gun and is heading to Washington. If the senator sees him in a crowd, he's supposed to duck."

The Senator was having an event at his house to which he had invited Governor Marvin Mandel of Maryland and an advance team of four Maryland state troopers descended on the house in McLean to check its security. They were impressed with the electrical room where all the telephone and electrical wires terminated. They were not impressed with his other lack of security. One issue was the windows in the entrance hall and gallery on the front of the house. As I recall, they did not have curtains. The troopers seemed concerned that a sniper could easily lie in wait at the top of the hill near the road and pick off a target in the house. "Isn't the senator concerned about a potential sniper?" asked the trooper. Dick's reply was simply to shrug and say what the senator had said many times before. "If someone wants to kill him, they will find a way to get to him. He isn't going to change his lifestyle on their account."

Once, however, when the office was at the height of turmoil as we were approaching the first anniversary of Bobby's death, with the reception room stuffed with people, the phones ringing off their hooks, and tourists waiting in the hall to catch a glimpse of the senator, a reporter whispered to me, "How long has Senator Kennedy had a bodyguard?"

I replied that he never has one. The reporter pointed to a man standing in the hall and said, "He has a gun. Isn't he a bodyguard?" At that moment the man made some kind of movement and I spotted a gun on his hip. I asked Dick what was going on and he said someone who had threatened the senator was thought to be in town. They were going to keep the guard on him until the memorial service for Bobby at Arlington a few days later. They figured since Vice President Agnew was attending, they could drop the guard then because the Secret Service would secure the cemetery.

And so it went.

Networking While Playing with the Owls

I was having the time of my life. The fall after the campaign, I moved into a townhouse on Kalorama Circle, just off Connecticut Avenue, to live with Carol Welch and Cassie Macken, who covered the White House for Hearst newspapers. Between them, they seemed to know just about everyone in Washington. We went into entertainment mode.

Never one to hide my candle under a bushel basket regardless of how weak the flame might be, when the girls asked if I could cook, I said, "Yes." What I really meant was that I was willing to learn. Since they weren't willing to do even that much, they became the cleanup team. They had the dirtiest end of that deal by far. We settled into a routine. They invited; I cooked.

Our first endeavor was a going away party for Angie Novello, who was off to Amsterdam with the State Department to get in her last year or two of government employment so she could have retirement benefits. Her invitation list was awesome, including as it did so many influential people in Washington. Our party was even mentioned in Maxine Cheshire's social column in the *Washington Post*, which gave us a presence in Washington, and we used it.

Although my hometown was the largest town on Maryland's Eastern

Shore, it had only about twenty thousand residents. Therefore, we were quite proud of ourselves when we successfully lured the National Indoor Tennis Tournament away from New York City's Madison Square Garden to play in our more modest civic center. We proudly wined and dined the players with some of them even staying in private homes. They seemed to enjoy themselves in our small arena where players and the audience were close enough to visit with each other.

Naturally, I bragged about it at work. As I prepared to go home for the weekend to see the games, Dick leaned back in his chair and, with a cocky little grin, asked me, "What do you all have for Thanksgiving down there in the sticks? Possum stuffed with acorns?"

"Actually, I prefer muskrat myself," I shot back at him indignantly.

Small as it was, Salisbury was still outside the Washington beltway, so the reporters were always eager to learn what the average person thought about what was happening in DC. Did they have opinions on current legislation? What were they talking about? Did they even care what was happening? I found they knew what was happening; they just didn't live and breathe politics as we did on the inside of the beltway.

Such was the case when once again my roommates and I were entertaining at yet another party. I was talking to Rollie Evans and Bob Novak, authors of a popular syndicated column, Evans & Novak, when they asked about my recent trip home to Salisbury for the tennis tournament. In fact, how did I think Senator Joe Tydings, Maryland's senator, was going to do in the upcoming election? Hmm, good question.

Well, my parents had had a tennis party after the championship match and the senator, who was staying with a mutual friend, accompanied his host to our party. It was unfortunate he dressed for the tennis tournament in his white V-neck tennis sweater, because, that being a much more formal time than now, the other men had dressed in coats and ties for the championship match and for our party. He stood out like a neon sign. But those things happen. What should not have happened is that he never sent a thank-you note to Mother and Dad. And that did not go down well.

So I told Rollie and Bob that I didn't think he was going to win. And to emphasize that point, I said that Dad had said he certainly wasn't going to vote for him. I'm not sure if it was Rollie or Bob who blurted out, "Your father, a member of the Democratic National Committee, isn't voting for Tydings!?" And before I could correct the error and say that an attorney in Salisbury named Wade Insley was the member, not Dad, someone pulled me away to handle an issue in the kitchen. I was impressed that national reporters such as Evans & Novak had such a depth of knowledge that they obviously knew who the elected members of the DNC from Maryland were, and presumably the other states as well, even if they did get the relationships wrong.

The absence of a thank-you note surprised me because Senator Kennedy was so careful about his own thank-yous. When he returned from an outing, party, or political function, he returned with a list of people to thank. The list was not just who had hosted him, but likely included who had created the flower arrangements on the tables or who had done some small task that might otherwise be overlooked. While he may not have handwritten the notes personally, he did have a designated person typing the notes on his personal stationery for his signature.

As with his attention to the needs of his constituents, I suspect the personal notes also went a long way toward helping him get reelected. So often it's the little things that mean the most. President George H. W. Bush once acknowledged being a prolific note writer. He attributed his success to those personal notes.

We loved to entertain. I have to admit we thought we were hot stuff. I was fearless in trying new dishes, my roommates were fearless in whom they invited to dinner. Eventually Wednesdays became Celebrity Night—like the Send a Kid to Camp program so widely advertised then, we had our Bring a Celebrity Home to Dinner program.

Celebrity Night began when Carol called me just before I was leaving work one Wednesday and asked about my plans for the evening. When I said I was so tired I was going to bed early, she exclaimed that they had invited Father Theodore Hesburgh to dinner. He was president of Notre Dame and recently had been appointed to the US Commission on Civil Rights. All I needed to do was stop by the grocery store and pick up some steaks, salad fixings, and some potatoes for baking—there would be ten of us for dinner at seven o'clock. And, indeed, they were there when I walked in with the groceries.

We had congressmen, presidential appointees, TV personalities, syndicated columnists, authors, and one dinner with George Christian, Frank Mankiewicz, and Dick Drayne (press secretaries for President Johnson, RFK, and EMK), as well as Dave Hackett, who had headed RFK's Boiler Room operation. Gary Hart came to dinner one evening and really impressed us. We declared he could go all the way if he didn't screw up—which was much more prophetic than we realized at the time.

I never served dessert; instead we had grasshoppers, a drink made with crème de menthe, crème de cacao, and ice cream. It became so popular that, instead of wine, guests would bring a half-gallon of ice cream to dinner.

Ethel had her eleventh child in December of 1968. Dick and I set up a press office at the hospital. No slouch in the baby delivery mode, Ethel arrived with her own satin sheets, pillows, and electric fan—along with her brother-in-law, who was going to be at her side during the delivery. Unfortunately for him she had a cesarean, and the senator nearly passed out.

Not long after Rory's birth, the staff and national press corps that had traveled on Robert Kennedy's campaign met for drinks and to share photos from the campaign. Someone commented that Ethel was probably feeling very blue following her delivery, and shouldn't we serenade her with Christmas carols some evening? Which we did—in the pouring rain. She invited us in to see the baby, and we all trooped up to her bedroom to wish her well. Thus caroling at Hickory Hill became an annual Christmas event for us.

We always celebrated Christmas in the office with a small eggnog party. Suddenly the roles were reversed. This was Methodist eggnog with no punch! Where were the Catholics when you needed them? Well, not to worry, I knew how to fix that. The senator had a cupboard with some whiskey, so each year I was the official eggnog spiker. One year I grabbed a bottle of cognac from his cupboard and upended the bottle over the punch bowl. The cognac was going *glug, glug, glug, glug* when I heard a gasp behind me. No need to check who was gasping, it could only be the owner of the bottle! Turning it up, I declared with a maestro's confidence, "That should do it." As I returned it to the cabinet, I checked the label a bit more carefully than I had when I chose it. It was a very old (and expensive) bottle of Courvoisier. It was very good eggnog that year.

Life was lively, to say the least. So I was startled one day to have a newcomer to Washington say, "what do you do for entertainment around here?" We were at a little neighborhood park letting our dogs run free. While the dogs played with each other, we chatted. He was with the new Nixon administration and had come from Massachusetts with former Governor Volpe, who had been designated secretary of transportation. "Are there any good restaurants around here? What do you do for fun? I've been here for several months, and my wife and I can't seem to get into the swing of things."

"Gosh," I replied, "there are lots of things to do here." And then I tried to come up with a suggestion. Well, after a little thought I realized we entertained ourselves with dinners and parties. He was with the Republicans and apparently, they didn't party very much.

President Nixon, a Quaker, had brought into his administration an unusually high number of Mormons, Baptists, and people of other Christian denominations who didn't drink. There had even been a big article in the social pages about the difficulty the ambassadors' wives were having entertaining the Nixon administration leaders because they didn't drink. How could they drink toasts when half the guests were not drinking champagne? Ginger ale apparently lost something in translation. I felt a little sorry for him and tried to suggest some restaurants he and his wife might try. But frankly, I wasn't very optimistic he was going to enjoy himself since it didn't seem the Republicans were having nearly the fun we were.

For one who enjoys fine dining, my dates with Mel, a local restaurateur, were delightful as well as informative. He introduced me to new restaurants and new cuisine. He also introduced me to his friend, Albert Sabin, the developer of the oral polio vaccine. The three of us had dinner one evening at a small Georgetown restaurant. Dr. Sabin was a wine connoisseur and, with eyes sparkling, he took the opportunity to instruct me on the finer qualities of various wines.

Turning to me, Dr. Sabin explained that one could predict the quality of a wine by examining the different characteristics of the cork, by checking the legs of the wine when swirling it in the glass, and by checking its clarity and color by holding it up to a light.

Then he and Mel began laughing as they reminisced about the time they had ordered a particularly fine bottle of wine.

"Do you remember when we turned down the wine because it was cloudy? And when the sommelier brought the second bottle, we held our glasses to the light again and that one was cloudy too?"

"What did you do that time?" I inquired.

"We sent it back again!" exclaimed Mel. Wondering why such a fine wine should be unacceptable, they discussed whether it may have been stored improperly as well as other possibilities. As they waited for the third bottle, they happened to notice the light at their table that they had used to check the clarity of the wine. To their horror, they laughed, the globe on the light was *frosted*. No wonder the wine seemed cloudy! They accepted the next bottle without comment.

Mel had a receding hairline that, apparently, he was a little self-conscious about, for he began wearing a toupee, which looked good on him. Sometimes I myself wore a wig when I was having a bad hair day, so we were quite a pair with our fake hair. Until, as we sat in his car one evening, our good-night kiss must have gotten a little carried away, for at some point Mel held up a furry thing and exclaimed, "What's this?"

We both reached for our heads, but alas, it was not his toupee but my wig he was holding up. I grabbed it, slammed it back on to my head, and beat a hasty retreat.

I had several wigs I occasionally wore to work. Eventually I stopped wearing them because I had a problem keeping them on my head.

There was a White Owl cigar commercial that was popular then. The White Owl spokeswoman was dressed all in feathers and had short, curly, white hair. While shopping with me one day, Mother spied a wig with short white curls similar to the White Owl woman; Mother encouraged me to buy it. So of course I did, silly me.

The first time I wore it to work, I had a number of comments from the staff and some members of the press. As I delivered some press releases to the press gallery in the Capitol, a couple of reporters exclaimed, "Loudell, what have you done?"

I laughed and assured them it wasn't permanent, it was just my wig.

Back at the office toward the end of the day, a number of us were standing around chatting when the senator walked into the room. He stared at me and was about to say something when I was called to the phone. As I spoke on the phone he pointed to my head and mouthed the same words as the reporters, "What have you done?"

When I hung up, I rejoined the huddle of people and, trying to reassure everyone, once again I said, "Oh, it isn't permanent, it's just a wig." And with that the senator reached over and gave it a playful tug. It was nearly off my head before he realized how loose it was. I grabbed it and pulled it back into place, but from then on when I wore a wig there was someone tugging on it. So I eventually stopped wearing those fashion statements.

Joan Kennedy

Joan Kennedy was a concert pianist, loved the arts, and supported the Washington Symphony Orchestra. When she and her family moved into the new home in McLean, Virginia, the press clamored to see it. Using that interest to her advantage, she had a party at her new home to promote the symphony's upcoming season and invited the press to cover it, which they were very happy to do. Press coverage included

Dick and me, of course. Wasn't this a wonderful job?

Their home was beautiful. As I recall, it overlooked the Great Falls of the Potomac River. It was a rancher with a strong Cape Cod influence. It was so cleverly built into the topography of the land, it appeared rather low-key. But inside it was much more spectacular. Now I'm doing this from memory so bear with me. In the entrance hallway, which, as I recall, extended as a gallery into the bedroom wing on the left side, were two beautiful antique corner cupboards. From there one went forward into a very large and dramatic living room. The ceiling was vaulted with massive oak beams supporting the roof. Here even the Kennedys had problems with builders, for after spending much time choosing just the right wood for the beams, which he intended to leave natural, the senator stopped by to check on the progress one day only to find the painter half-finished painting the beams white! Even so the ceiling was dramatic. The glass doors that opened onto the deck were oversized, much taller than average, and when opened they stacked up on themselves like pocket doors, leaving a very wide opening to the deck and the view of the rapids.

On the piano in the living room was a large vase with a mass of flowers. I had arrived early to help with any last-minute details when Joan arrived from, judging by her wardrobe, horseback riding. She walked in, surveyed everything, tweaked the flowers in the arrangement, and turned to go change for the party. I commented on the flower arrangement, and she observed that it was now several days old. She said she had learned from her mother-in-law how to extend the "life" of such an expensive arrangement by simply replacing the dead flowers with silk ones. As I watched her leave to dress for the party, I wondered if I'd ever reach a point where I could simply arrive for my own party, tweak a few things, and be ready. Well, so far it hasn't happened!

Chappaquiddick

In March or April, Dave Hackett gave a party as a belated thank-you for the Boiler Room girls. He invited two young single men for each of the women and had his son's band play at the party. The senator attended and had a wonderful time. At some point, he and Mary Ellen Lyons went driving around town while he reminisced about his brother, Bobby. When the party finally broke up at four in the morning, he declared himself too drunk to drive and insisted someone drive him home.

He had had such a good time (in fact, it was the first fun party he'd attended since his brother's death) that nothing would do but that he should also give the Boiler Room girls a party as a token of appreciation for their hard work in his brother's campaign. And why not have it during the Edgartown Regatta in July? He had his cousin, Joey Gargan, set it up on Chappaquiddick Island, where there could be some privacy. (It was customary for us to have office parties in out-of-the-way places so tourists weren't hanging around. Whether it was a Christmas party or some other event, dates were not welcome; only spouses could attend these functions.)

As it happened, that was the same weekend that America's astronauts were landing on the moon for the first time, so reporters were constantly checking with us to see where the senator would be that weekend in order to get a statement from him. Everyone knew about the party.

And everywhere in the world there were moon-landing parties. The girls were bummed out that they would have to attend what was shaping up to be a very boring party, since none of the men were dating material, while their friends would be attending fun parties elsewhere.

That weekend I was home explaining to Mother that I thought

it was time to leave the senator and maybe move to Atlanta. It had been a year since the presidential campaign, and I thought EMK was where he was happiest and most effective and would not ever run for the presidency—at least not anytime soon. We were discussing what a wonderful experience it had been for me, and I had just said, "The nice thing about the Kennedys is you can always count on them to do the right thing, at least socially, even if one didn't always like their politics."

And as those words were hanging in the air, a news bulletin was broadcast on the television, which was on in the den. The announcer said there was an APB issued for the arrest of Senator Edward M. Kennedy in connection with leaving the scene of an accident in Chappaquiddick that had resulted in the death of his passenger, a young woman who had been on his brother's staff.

Naturally I was horrified. This most definitely was *not* socially correct.

When I finally got over the fact that a friend had been killed, and the victim had been identified as Mary Jo, I assured Mother that at least there could be no scandal attached to her, she was a straight arrow from the word go.

This showed how much I still had to learn about how the press can distort things.

Nance Lyons told me later that the party had been just as boring as she had feared it would be—not much drinking and certainly not a lot of revelry. The men were friends of Joey's; even Jack Crimmins was a guest, who to us seemed ancient. Relatively early in the evening, the senator had said he was leaving and asked if anyone wanted a ride back to Edgartown. Mary Jo, who was never one for a lot of partying, accepted.

EMK said he made a wrong turn onto the dirt road that led to the fateful bridge. But I have always wondered if he didn't start reminiscing about his brother, Bobby, and simply decided to drive and talk for a while. With death such a constant companion for him, I think he was so totally unable to handle being the cause of someone else's death that he made quite a number of awful decisions that evening.

Here's my take on it:

Because he swam every day to strengthen his back, which he had broken in an airplane crash in 1964, he was very comfortable in the water. Plus he was holding on to the steering wheel, which would have helped orient himself upside down in the dark water. Mary Jo had no such orientation and she was extremely uncomfortable in the water, and so probably she did not survive very long submerged in an overturned car with an open window that had water gushing in.

I believe he would have tried to dive several times to find her, just as he testified, but the current was quite swift then, and he really didn't have much of a chance of finding her.

Never one to have any money in his pocket, he couldn't call from the public phone that was nearby. And it was totally consistent with his thinking to find people he knew to help him rather than to knock on a stranger's door late at night.

Being an Irish male chauvinist at the time, which I had come to believe were worse than most other men, he naturally turned to the men at the party—the very ones who were *not* advisors, who instead always waited for him to tell them what to do. Even when they were back at the accident site, they relied on him to make decisions, never considering that he might be in shock and thinking poorly.

The Boiler Room girls were made of stronger stuff. If he'd gone to them, they would have very likely taken charge of the situation and called for help, which is what the average person does when coming upon an accident. They would be the ones to call the authorities while the victim sits in shock by the side of the road wondering how it happened.

And once the senator swam from Chappaquiddick to Edgartown, I think he simply could not face what had happened and hid from this new nightmare.

Be that as it may, there was a big mess to handle. And obviously this wasn't the time to leave, for if I did, I feared the press would interpret my leaving in some negative fashion.

There wasn't much for us to do the first week after the accident because the senator remained on the Cape, saying nothing. His house was not in the famous Kennedy Compound, so the first thing he did was to move to his brother Jack's place, which was protected from the press. Dave Burke, the senator's chief of staff, and Loretta Cubberly from the office (who took my place when I eventually left) were there with other advisors.

Dun Gifford, from our office, was dispatched to pick up Mary Jo's body and return it to her parents. I guess they didn't use body bags in those days, because a picture of him showed her obviously contorted blanket-draped body on a stretcher as it was taken from a private plane. That must have been an awful experience for Dun, to sit in the tight confines of a small plane next to the skimpily covered body of someone he knew.

Dave would call the office and speak to Dick a couple times a day. But he called from a public phone booth just outside the compound, saying he feared that President Kennedy's phones were tapped. I scoffed at such paranoia. Didn't the president's house have the much-touted White House communications system? Shouldn't it be secure? The system wasn't antiquated; after all, it had been only six years since the president's death. Even so, the people there seemed fixated on the notion they were being spied on.

It was decided that the senator would not make any statement until after Mary Jo's funeral. And that seemed to take forever. At one point, with everyone waiting around for the funeral, there was simply no breaking news. Dick quipped that the *Daily News* and the *New York Post* were probably frantic for something to write—that he fully expected to see a headline, "Blonde Still Dead," just to fill the space.

Even now whenever there is a scandal and the press is hot on the scent, but there's no breaking news because the prosecutor is mum or the police have nothing to share and the press needs a headline, I find myself looking for those "Blonde Still Dead" headlines—"Police Have No New Clues" or "Prosecutor Silent."

As bad as the press was at the time, and to me they seemed awful, they were nowhere near as bad as they are today. At least then they had daily deadlines, not minute-by-minute deadlines as they have now with twenty-four-hour coverage constantly needing fresh meat. With all the negative coverage, EMK complained only once, about an article in *Ladies Home Journal* saying that he'd been kicked out of his bed and was sleeping on the sofa.

The first time EMK appeared in public after the accident was at Mary Jo's funeral. It would have helped a lot if he'd had a broken bone or at least a scratch somewhere on his face. He looked none the worse for wear—except for a neck collar, which simply made him appear to be looking for sympathy. He'd have been better off without it, and in fact, he never wore it again in public.

Then it was time for his address to the citizens of Massachusetts, probably the most important speech of his career. It was carried nationally on all the networks. Loretta had been doing secretarial duty at the compound and had been charged with finding a thesaurus. Finally locating one at Rose Kennedy's house, she slipped over to pick it up, only to have the senator's mother poke her head over the second floor banister to say, "You just remember where you got that. And be sure to bring it back when you're finished with it." There was a mother with priorities.

After the speech, which received mixed reviews, the senator went into seclusion until the coroner's inquest. He was found guilty of leaving the scene of an accident. Being a first offender, he got probation and his driver's license was suspended.

Finally, he was ready to return to work. As I arrived at the office door that morning, there sat several photographers and reporters camped out in the hall waiting for him. When they told me what they were there for, I explained that they should go to the Capitol's steps, as that was where he was to arrive for a photo op. Indeed, two to three hundred of the press corps watched as he walked up the steps. The headlines around the world reported, "Kennedy Returns to Work."

That evening as we were closing the office, Andy Vitalli came up to me and asked where my car was. I told him, "Downstairs. Why?"

"Well," he said with a sheepish smile, "we were so concerned this morning about having someone drive the senator to work and get him to the Capitol on time that no one thought about how to get him home."

Now it was time for him to leave, and he had no ride.

Could Andy drive the senator home in my car and then return to get me? I could then drive him back to the senator's house in McLean, where Andy had left his own car that morning. Being the compassionate, understanding staff member that I was, I said, "Hell, no."

With that scenario, I would be terribly late for my date; besides, I had agreed to drive someone else home from the office. But she and I could drive the senator to his house, which would be no problem. "Yes, it would," Andy said, cringing. If the press saw not one but two women alone in a car with him, it's hard to imagine how awful the headlines would be!

But I was the only option so we finally reached a compromise. Andy would drive the senator home in my car with Jane and me riding as passengers in the backseat. As the four of us were descending in the Senate elevator, the Senator half chuckled, half grimaced as he said, "If the press only knew; here's the real story: not that I returned to work, but that I couldn't get home!"

Vice President Agnew Voices His Opinion

With the senator back at work, we resumed entertaining. I guess our parties were getting something of a reputation, as representatives for Alaska's native groups approached us about helping them with their lobbying. Their proposal was that, if we would invite one hundred of our nearest and dearest friends to a party at our house so they could talk to them, they would pay for the food and drinks.

Carol and Cassie, looking at me with eager little smiles, said something along the lines of: "That wouldn't be any trouble for you to do, would it, Loudell?"

"Think what a coup this would be!"

"We'll help, of course."

So on a chilly evening in October, we had a big party with a guest list of mostly news media and political activists, which actually were the only type of people we knew. There were people from *Time, Life, Look,* the *Washington Post,* the *New York Times,* the *Boston Globe,* the *Boston Herald,* CBS, ABC, and NBC—columnists, newspaper publishers, freelance writers, and, of course, Senator Kennedy.

The lobbyists were delighted. They were meeting and talking to more people in one night than they could ordinarily reach in weeks. We were delighted. We were showing off, and it wasn't costing us anything.

Describing the news media and others as "pointy-headed liberals" and "nattering nabobs," Vice President Agnew had for some time been turning up the heat on the Democrats and the national media until it was now reaching the boiling point. On the night of our party he was to give a speech in Des Moines, Iowa, attacking the TV network anchors as being biased and too liberal. It was to be carried live on all the networks. The party stopped when the speech began. Just like a Super Bowl game, everyone gathered around to watch. When Agnew finished, there was a moment of stunned silence, and then a babble of indignation erupted. We were staggered by the enormity of the attack.

Quite obviously, we needed to rebut this. And there in the same room stood the press and the senator, ready to go on the offensive. Dick and the senator were whispering and I gravitated toward them. Dick asked if there was a typewriter in the house; I said, yes, I had one in my bedroom. Then Dick raised his hands for attention and announced to everyone that the senator would have a statement for them in a just few minutes.

We three trooped to my room, huddled around the typewriter,

and as Dick and the senator dictated, I typed a one-page statement in response to the vice president's accusations. As the party continued, everyone passed the single sheet of paper around the living room, and each reporter copied what he needed, passing the release along to his competitor when finished. Then they took turns at the only phone in the house calling in their stories. The party never missed a beat. The very idea—saying the media was not objective!

In 1968 a group of reporters who had covered Robert Kennedy's campaign created the Robert F. Kennedy Award for Excellence in Journalism in his honor. In addition to the speeches, the dinner and the recognition of the award winner, there was also musical entertainment.

The senator, who loved music, was trying to help the organizers book the entertainment. We were all standing around outside his office while he tried to reach Art Garfunkel in Mexico, where he was working on a film. We could hear him because his door was open and he was almost shouting as he tried to get through to whoever answered the phone in Mexico that he was Senator Kennedy trying to reach Art Gar*finkel*. (Garfinkel's was an upscale department store in DC.) "Garfinkel," he said even louder, "have Garfinkel call me at this number." We were all chuckling over his once again messing up someone's name while at the same time anticipating the coup we would achieve if we could book Simon & Garfunkel for the awards dinner.

By the next day, the return call had still not come in when I pulled Dick aside and asked him if they had considered that Simon & Garfunkel would surely be expected to perform their current big hit, "Bridge Over Troubled Water." Apparently, they had not, for he blanched and bolted for the inner sanctum. Simon & Garfunkel did not perform at the awards dinner.

One day sometime in the winter of 1969-1970 Dick and I were

waiting for the elevator in the Senate office building when Dave Burke walked by with his hands in his pockets looking like he was carrying the weight of the world on his shoulders. Dick called him over and asked what was going on.

Dave was just leaving the mail room where he had been tracking down a missing letter from a witness to the My Lai massacre perpetrated by American soldiers in Viet Nam. My Lai was a huge story then and one that the House Armed Services Committee was trying to cover up. The writer claimed publicly he had sent Senator Kennedy and many other politicians a certified letter revealing what took place there. It had been mimeographed. He had never heard from any of them, including Senator Kennedy.

Dave had found the certified mail form that a volunteer had signed but not the letter. *Oh, dear. Oh, dear.* He said something like "it could have helped us." Then he turned and continued walking to his office.

Turning to Dick I asked what the Senator could have done. He replied, "The Senator could have held hearings on what happened at My Lai. We could have used it to quick start his rehabilitation after Chappaquiddick."

As Dick was explaining this, in my mind's eye, I was watching myself as I threw the letter into the trash. Two words in the letter burned into my head: My Lai.

I was stunned. I'm not sure what my reaction would have been because just then I heard a voice in my head. Not my own, it was one I did not recognize. It said very calmly, *"You saved his life."* Suddenly I was comforted, at peace and not feeling a bit of guilt. The elevator bell dinged, Dick and I turned and entered it.

There were times when we women in the office, and I surely led the chorus, were upset that when there was a "staff memo," it was meant just for the men—not for the women. Once there was even a "staff" meeting in Boston just for the men. I looked around the office, and seeing only women, I rebelled. Working under the old adage that when the cat's away the mice can play, I went through the office gathering anyone and everyone who was game and we headed out to a very long lunch. In fact it became so long that we never went back to the office that day. It was so long that the restaurant ran out of those cute little coconut shells they were serving the piña coladas in. It was so long that the message might have actually been received, because I don't recall ever again seeing a "staff memo" that excluded women.

It's Time to Go

Family was important to Ted Kennedy. The senator took his responsibilities very seriously in his role as father to sixteen children—three children of his own plus thirteen in his extended family. Many times someone on the staff could be seen outside his office door long after six o'clock waiting for the senator to finish telling one of his children a bedtime story over the phone. Or at Halloween, he accompanied his kids as they went door to door trick-or-treating, with him disguised as a ghost. Or he might be talking to a headmaster about his nephew Joe Kennedy's poor grades. His mother sent memos to all the family reminding them to keep in touch with Rosemary, their institutionalized sister, and Ted did so.

With spring's arrival came another period of introspection, and what I saw didn't please me. I don't recall what comment or what event made me pause and take a long look at myself, but I did. It was as if God's hand on my shoulder had turned me around and said, "Take a look at what you have become. Are you happy with this result? Is this what you want to be?"

The power and prestige of my association with the Kennedys was heady stuff and I had become impressed with myself and my influence, forgetting that the real power originated with the senator. Arrogance is not a good characteristic, and I had indeed become haughty.

If something didn't happen as I expected it to—a repairman wasn't available immediately, or someone or something would not be arriving when I expected—it was totally unacceptable, and I became rather obnoxious in my indignation. I was quick to tell the offender what I thought and what they should do about it.

It's easy when one lives in the rarified air reserved for one's circle of friends and colleagues to believe that you know more than others. That your position on issues is the correct one—all others are wrong. From our lofty, superior positions, my friends and I would snicker and scoff at those we deemed to be less than we were, and we found almost everyone inferior.

At parties I had become the all-knowing one with the inside track on what was really happening in Congress. With a smug smile or an arched brow (well, it would have been arched if I could move my eyebrows), I let my audience know that I knew what they could never really know, because I, Loudell, lived and breathed on the inside track. Where they did not.

Spring is the time for fresh evaluations and renewals. Once again I reassessed myself and didn't like what I saw. Even though at the time I couldn't pinpoint what was wrong, I knew I didn't like what I had become. It was time to get out of that environment, to move on. To what, I wasn't certain. But moving on felt like the right thing to do. Besides, I was still prepared to jump in front of speeding bullets to save the senator. And that was definitely not a healthy attitude!

I looked south, to Atlanta. Since college it seemed to be my escape route of choice, for leaving the Hill and working elsewhere in town had absolutely no appeal to me. During a week's vacation, my cousin, Fran Campbell, took me in hand and guided me through the intricacies of job and apartment hunting. Eventually I found a position as executive secretary at Tucker Wayne, an advertising agency. And I put a deposit on an apartment that looked like a concrete bunker but was in the Piedmont section of Atlanta, an area that had Fran's approval.

My decision to move on came as a surprise to everyone. It wasn't easy telling Dick and my roommates that I was leaving. Dick walked me down the hall and said, "You know, if I asked you to stay, you would, wouldn't you?"

"Yes," I agreed, "I would if you asked me to. But I do think it's time for me to go."

There was a good deal of leave-taking involved, with going-away parties and engraved mementos from some of the media, personally autographed pictures from the senator, autographed books by some friendly reporters, as well as an article in the paper noting that Dun Gifford and I were leaving Senator Kennedy, "...yet another indication that his presidential hopes had been ended by his accident." So much for trying to avoid a negative news article about the senator's presidential prospects.

My time on the Hill had been so precious to me. Every day I pinched myself to be sure I wasn't dreaming. To be in the middle or, more often, on the fringes, of historical events as they occurred had been beyond any dreams I could have imagined. It hurt to leave there, but at the same time, it was exciting to move on to other chapters in my life. As I left, I reminisced about the events that had occurred during the five years I had worked for Ted Kennedy.

There had been two births: Patrick Kennedy in 1967 to Ted and Joan; and Rory Kennedy to Ethel in 1968.

There had been a presidential campaign.

There had been three deaths: the assassination of Robert Kennedy and the equivalent of a state funeral; the accidental death of Mary Jo Kopechne and attendant scandal; and the death of Ambassador Joseph P. Kennedy, the senator's father.

There had been the wedding of Jacqueline Kennedy Onassis.

And one small political victory, the senator's election to the post of Senate whip.

I'd been there for the christening of the aircraft carrier *John F. Kennedy*, I had flown on and later attended the decommissioning of the *Caroline*, President Kennedy's famous plane. I had been with EMK from the time he had been a very junior, albeit famous, senator from Massachusetts to a power to be reckoned with in the US Senate. I had been there to watch firsthand as the senator overcame tragedies and hurdles that would have caused lesser men to give up. I had been there as he found his stride, and himself, and the issues that would make him a force in Washington for years to come. I had watched him as he persevered year after year to pass legislation he believed in. Perhaps one year he'd get a half loaf and then another year a slice, compromising when and where he had to, until eventually, over time, he ended up with what he wanted.

I had also learned that each of us, whether we be high and mighty or low and dirty, were not very different in the long run. The mighty could be just as hurt, embarrassed, happy, and caring, or as foolish and disappointing, as the average person. But most importantly, I learned that one person with a passion for an issue could make a difference.

Finally, I turned in my key and identification card, said my last good-byes, and headed toward the door. The phone rang and rang, so I turned and answered it one last time. It was a black mother calling from South Carolina. Her son had been killed in Vietnam and buried in her hometown. She had missed making some payments on his cemetery plot and the owner had dug up her son's casket and dumped it on her doorstep. *Could the senator help?* I handed the phone to a staffer and left. I was sure going to miss all this.

A mover's representative had come to the house to give me an estimate. Mother told me later he had looked at my photos of Senator Kennedy and made a snide comment about him that surprised even her. Incensed, I picked up the phone, called his manager, and told him in no uncertain terms what I thought of his employee making such comments about my boss. See, I really did need to get out of there.

CHAPTER FIVE

BEYOND CAPITOL HILL—A DIFFERENT WORLD

*Getting fired is nature's way of telling you that
you had the wrong job in the first place.*
—Hal Lancaster

Atlanta was a totally different scene from DC. It was a young city; in fact, there were so many young people there that, at age twenty-nine, I felt old. It was a fun place with something happening all the time. In comparison, Washington seemed like a town with a serious old-fogey attitude.

My position at Tucker Wayne was in the rarified air of the executive suite, as secretary to both the chairman of the board and the executive vice president. Accustomed as I was to working under pressure for long hours, I knew from the first day I was in serious trouble.

Between the two men, they generated little or no work for me. And, unfortunately, early on when the chairman dictated a lengthy memo with a lot of advertising terms I was unfamiliar with, my shorthand failed miserably. Not a good beginning; things plunged downhill from there.

Matt Conner, the chairman of the board, had read somewhere that it was important to set a good example for one's employees by arriving at the office early and being seen among the last to leave in the evening. And that's exactly what he did. Our hours were nine to five o'clock. So he was at his desk by 8:30 in the morning and still there when we left work at five. However, he played tennis from ten to two o'clock every day. And during the six-month period they had been without a secretary the vice president had learned to fend for himself, so he had little or nothing for me to do. Consequently, I had about a half day's worth of work each week! I spent a lot of time brushing up on shorthand. Life at Tucker Wayne was boring.

However, what little excitement there was at work was more than made up for at my apartment building. Life there was like a soap opera. I could hardly wait to get home each day to hear what new scandals were in the air.

My three-story apartment building was built into the side of a small hill and overlooked the road below. Parking was behind the building, and one reached one's apartment by either walking up an open flight of steps or down a flight-and-a-half to the lower level, or in my case, half a flight down to the middle level. Each stairwell had a total of six units opening onto it.

The building was built totally of concrete; it felt and looked like a fortress and gave one a sense of being securely enveloped in a safe little cocoon, albeit a hard one. It seemed as if the world could throw its worst at this building, and it would be impervious. I felt very safe.

In addition to the building itself, I also had my personal protectors. Across the hall on my level was a young woman whose husband was serving in Vietnam. She owned a white German shepherd, who she assured me had been trained to kill on command. Should anyone even think of breaking into her unit, this mighty beast would rip his throat out on her command, and I could be sure that she would not hesitate to give the order. Apparently, I looked like a nice-enough person, for the dog's owner decided that she would extend the "safe circle" to include my apartment as well. So if I should ever need any help, just shout and she'd sic her dog on any miscreant who was bothering me.

Below was a recycled bachelor, a vice president of a local bank. These were his interim quarters while he tied up the loose ends of his divorce, licked his not-so-deep wounds, and reentered the dating scene. He assured me he had an arsenal of guns, including some that were semiautomatics; I had only to knock three times on the floor, and he'd be there in a minute to protect me. It took me a while to stop tiptoeing around my apartment for fear of inadvertently sending a signal that I needed help.

Jack, my recycled bachelor, was apparently already testing the dating waters at an apartment complex just down the street from us, for there was often a woman (I'm not certain it was always the same one) standing on the knoll under his window calling to him. "Jack, Jack, are you there? I need you." Eventually Jack would answer her, and I could hear her as she went down the steps to his apartment. He swore with a straight face he was only helping her through some difficult times—that one o'clock in the morning was often a particularly challenging time for her.

If Jack wasn't helping damsels in distress, he was loaning out his sofa to his friends who were temporarily or permanently estranged from their wives. There was constant traffic around his apartment.

Across the hall from Jack on the lower level were some newlyweds who we seldom saw. Above me was a young woman who frequently had someone sleep over, but not always. And across from her was a young couple who had a storefront dress shop in Atlanta, not very far from our building. They came and went at odd hours of the day.

One night around one o'clock I heard a noise under the window and then a voice calling for Jack. Nothing new here, except that I began to notice other voices and there was that flashing blue light coming in my windows, so I wandered onto my balcony to check things out.

Lying on the ground with a number of people circling her was my upstairs neighbor, who had fallen off her balcony, smashing her heel on my balcony as she passed it on the way to hitting the ground under Jack's window. Eventually she was taken by ambulance to the hospital for a little repair work.

The next day my across-the-hall neighbor filled me in. Apparently, the woman was sitting on the edge of her balcony drinking with her boyfriend when, slightly inebriated, she leaned back and fell off.

The day after that, Jack corrected the story. Apparently, the woman's boyfriend was the Local Mafia Representative (he made it sound like this was a franchise situation) and the woman was a hooker he had set up in the apartment upstairs. Unfortunately for her, the Local Mafia Representative believed she had been getting a little too close to the husband of the couple next door to her, so the Local Mafia Representative taught her a lesson by pushing her off the balcony.

I exclaimed over the idea she was a hooker, and Jack assured me that not only was she one, but her friends who had come to her aid when she fell were also hookers who lived at the other end of our building. I was dumbfounded. He said, "Haven't you ever noticed the number of cars driving through here? They're the johns looking for the girls."

I had no idea!

A couple of days later when I was leaving for work, my across-the-hall neighbor stopped me as she was walking her killer dog to exclaim over the latest news. Her upstairs neighbors' dress store had caught fire the previous night and they had lost everything.

People at work were suitably enthralled with my neighbors' on-going sagas. And there in the newspaper was an article about the fire, which the paper described as arson. The store was next door to the campaign headquarters of Julian Bond, an up-and-coming black politician, and there was speculation that the arsonist had intended to firebomb Bond's offices and had hit my neighbor's place by mistake.

When I returned home that evening, my neighbor was walking her dog again; how else could she keep track of everything? She confided to me that the arsonist had not been mistaken; apparently the Local Mafia Representative was teaching another lesson, this time to the husband across the way from his little love nest: "Keep your hands off my woman."

However, the final chapter was written when I saw Jack the following day, and I exclaimed over the mafia lessons being taught upstairs. He shook his head and defended the Local Mafia Representative. Once again, my neighbor's story needed correcting. The Local Representative had not been out teaching lessons after all, for when the police had arrived to inform the couple upstairs their business had been burned and they had lost everything, the husband answered the door with scorched arms and had been immediately arrested for burning his own business to get the insurance money!

For me, Atlanta's difference lay in the lifestyles of the people I knew there. In Washington, my friends and I were particularly careful about where we went, what we did, and what the other people who were with us did. Heaven forbid we should be associated with anything that might smack of scandal.

In Washington I was so circumspect with my dates that one observed to a mutual friend after a date that he was halfway to the lobby before he realized he wasn't spending the night with me. In Atlanta, on the other hand, my dates were in the door and stripping before I could turn around.

In Atlanta, who cared? This city offered anonymity that Washington had not. At work, a group of men went to lunch at a topless Japanese stir-fry restaurant that had just opened. When I inquired how lunch was, one of the married men replied, "Well, stir-fry dishes are awfully hot and steamy, and it kind of took my appetite away when the topless waitress had beads of sweat dripping off her boob into my food!"

I couldn't help but be struck by the number of black people I was thrown with, both at work and in social situations, as compared to Washington. In DC., we were vigilant concerning the rights of oppressed minorities, but we didn't know many—and certainly not to socialize with. Occasionally my roommates and I would say we needed to invite some black people to our parties, but we didn't even know any to invite. There was only one black person in our office, hired not long before I left. In Atlanta, however, the black people I met held good positions in the business world and were guests in my friends' homes and at parties.

Alas, things didn't work out well at Tucker Wayne and eventually the vice president and I had our longest conversation of my tenure there. During the course of this conversation, it occurred to me that I was being fired. He was being so gentle and kind that I began making mental notes of his technique in case I should ever be in a position to fire someone myself.

Having seen the handwriting on the wall for some time, I had already been testing the job-market waters, but having been given notice, I began job hunting in earnest. It wasn't for lack of job offers that I returned to Washington; it was the lack of a decent wage in Atlanta and the offer of a position with the Peace Corps in Washington that did the trick.

In the Peace Corps—But Not as a Volunteer

The world had been turning while I was away and, though I kept up my friendships from before, I moved into an efficiency apartment that seemed to be in the high-crime/low-rent district of Connecticut Avenue, not far from my former Kalorama townhouse and near the Hilton Hotel (where President Reagan was nearly assassinated some years later). During the riots following Martin Luther King Jr.'s death, parts of the area not far from where I now lived were burned. While moving into my new apartment, the mover's ten-year-old son went to the corner store across the street from my building with a five-dollar bill in his hand and came back crying because some bigger boys had roughed him up and taken his money. Welcome back.

Created by President Kennedy, the Peace Corps prided itself on a nonpartisan spirit that the first director, Sargent Shriver, had insisted upon at its inception. The Peace Corps was established about the time I graduated from college and I had thoughts then about becoming a volunteer but never followed through. Now I was a mercenary in the Peace Corps, working in Washington in the press office and getting paid a decent wage.

To celebrate the corps' tenth anniversary, the US Postal Service had agreed to issue a stamp commemorating the milestone. We invited everyone in the country to participate in a contest to design the stamp: elementary students, art majors, commercial artists, and amateur and professional photographers submitted artwork and photographs for the national contest. The photos were to be judged by nationally renowned

Beyond Capitol Hill—A Different World

photographers; the winning poster would become the stamp.

The whole event culminated in a show at the Smithsonian Institution where we displayed all the thousands of posters that were submitted and the hundreds and hundreds of photographs that volunteers had taken in the remote areas of the world where they had served. The opening of the show was a cocktail party for invited guests, the press, the board of advisors of the Peace Corps, and various staff members; the highlight of the evening was the announcement of the winners.

The winning stamp design for the Peace Corps' tenth anniversary.

Mother came to the event. She was suitably impressed, not just by the displays, but also by the compliments I received from several reporters there who were friends of mine from the Hill. Sometimes I felt she never really believed I did what I said I did when I worked for the senator.

I was enormously proud of Mother when we had reached the far end of the hall of posters. It was just us and one other person there admiring the artwork. As the three of us turned to retrace our steps down the very long corridor, Mother struck up a conversation with our companion, Neil Armstrong, as comfortably as if she'd known him for years. As I wondered frantically what we could talk about for the entire length of this walk, Mother began with, "And how's the family?" With that there was never a pause in their conversation. Neil Armstrong slowed his pace to match Mother's, something Dad rarely did, and they chatted for nearly ten minutes as they walked. My only regret is that I didn't get a photo of her with the first man to walk on the moon.

Meanwhile there were drumbeats of change pounding the agency. The Nixon administration was determined to place the Peace Corps, AmeriCorps, SCORE, and other domestic volunteer organizations into one large agency, to be called ACTION. It would also become a partisan agency, which almost everyone in the Peace Corps opposed.

Washington is such a partisan town, with the administration in power filling political vacancies with party loyalists, that to have any agency above the partisan fray was a tremendous advantage for those who worked there. One obvious benefit was not worrying about one's party affiliation. Every governmental agency and department have some top-level people who are presidential appointees, and thus are replaced as the president is replaced. If, however, the other agency positions were not affected by one's party affiliation, then presumably, if one did a good job, one could continue on even if the party in power changed.

Or at least that's what I thought.

And since the FBI had interviewed Dick in the senator's office when they were conducting my background check for the Peace Corps position, I believed my Democratic party affiliation was not a problem, or I would never have been hired. Thus, when I joined with nineteen other friends in renting an estate in McLean, Virginia, for the summer, it never occurred to me to be concerned about job security. These were Kennedy people or friends in the media such as Dick Drayne, Carol Welch, Cassie Macken (then with ABC), Terry Smith (then with the *New York Times,* later with public broadcasting); Tom Scanlon, a former Peace Corps volunteer and Carol's boyfriend (who was our connection with Father Hesburgh); Anne Wexler (a feminist); Ed and Loretta Cubberly, and others.

One of the ground rules at the house was that I was off-limits for everyone as a source of information about the Peace Corps. The fact that Tom was testifying before Senator Kennedy's subcommittee in opposition to the creation of ACTION, or that Cassie and Terry were covering the hearings for their respective organizations, or that I had my own connections with both the Peace Corps and the Kennedys, did not faze me in the least.

Once when I was a teenager with a perplexing question about what to do in some situation, Mother had answered me with a quotation from Shakespeare:

> *This above all: to thine own self be true, and it must follow, as the night the day, Thou canst not then be false to any man.*
> —*Shakespeare, Hamlet*

And that is what I've tried to do all my life. My philosophy was that while I worked for the Peace Corps, my loyalty was to the Peace Corps. Everyone seemed comfortable with that and I never gave it another thought, even when the *New York Times* began printing leaks from the Peace Corps.

I felt so protected by the nonpartisanship of the Peace Corps that I didn't even hesitate in telling sweet, grandmotherly Betty Williams, who was assistant to the director of the agency, some little thing that happened on Robert Kennedy's campaign. She was clearly startled that I had been associated with the Kennedys. It wasn't long before I began to sense some bad vibes as I made my way around the agency. So many bad vibes that I asked Jack Porter, my boss, if we could have lunch; we had to talk. Over lunch, I asked him for work that would give me a much lower profile around the office because I was beginning to feel like a turkey at a turkey shoot, and it wasn't a good feeling.

Jack said it was too late. Betty had apparently gone straight to Director Blatchford to tell him of my Kennedy connections. Jack had just spent ninety minutes in the personnel department trying to save me my job and had failed. He had been told to fire me. He did ask if I was the source for the *New York Times*, and I assured him I was not. I explained that my friends and I had agreed I would be off-limits, and so we never spoke of the Peace Corps.

Jack went on to say that it was most amazing how much the personnel director knew about my life. For one thing, he knew everything about the house in McLean, even down to the names of everyone who had bought into our little rental plan. He knew who I'd had dates with and much more. The man had recently come over to the Peace Corps personnel office from the Department of Justice, which, under the direction of Attorney General John Mitchell, had a reputation for being vicious. He was ready to clean the house of anyone with a connection to the Kennedys, so I had to go.

But more importantly, Jack said, he knew much more about me and my friends than was normal for a person in his position. Jack had been a top executive in a large advertising firm in New York before becoming director of public relations for the Peace Corps, and if he said it was scary what they knew and was very concerned for me, then I was alarmed.

After all was said and done, I was fired. Happy thirtieth birthday.

I went home and huddled in a corner, crying and licking my wounds. The good news was that I had been given thirty days' notice; the bad news was I had to go into the office and work for those thirty days. After a couple of days of high tension, people talking in whispers, my long face, and a generally demoralized office, I was told to go home and not come back. They would pay me anyway. Then I went home to Mother and Dad and let them comfort me.

It wasn't long, however, before I was back looking at help-wanted ads. I still had our miniresort in McLean where I was surrounded by friends, who were generally commenting about how spooky Nance Lyons had felt after Chappaquiddick when her roommate, Mary Jo, had died. Nance had been certain that her phones were tapped and someone had been watching her place. I had previously pooh-poohed that notion, but now I wasn't so sure—especially when people were saying there might be something to Jack's comments about their knowing too much about me. Then they would bring up, once again, the fears of the phones being tapped in Hyannis Port while the senator was up there working on his post-Chappaquiddick speech. All in all, we settled into a paranoid period, swapping stories over dinner.

CHAPTER SIX

MESS WITH DEMOCRACY, GO TO JAIL

Democracy is two wolves and a lamb voting on what to have for lunch. Liberty is a well-armed lamb contesting the vote!
—Benjamin Franklin

Eventually I found myself back at the senator's office, where maybe lightning would strike twice. After all, it was there I had run into Dan Blackburn with his offer of a job at the Peace Corps. And I did have a bone to pick. While sitting in the office telling everyone they needed to help me find a new job (since it was my connection with the senator that had cost me this last one), Joe Mohbat, who covered national politics for the AP, mentioned that the director for the Democratic National Convention, Dick Murphy, was looking for a secretary. Joe not only set up the appointment for me; he sat in on the interview.

Once again, I assured a future employer I knew shorthand, but also that I could not be bought, which seemed very important to Dick.

Because the 1968 convention in Chicago had been such a disaster, with hundreds of unauthorized people gaining access to the floor with Dick Tuck's bogus credentials, Dick Murphy was determined to prevent

Mess with Democracy, Go to Jail

any possibility of a recurrence. I assured him I was a Girl Scout through and through, a tower of strength against the tides of temptation, and that never, never would I ever consider allowing anyone to have, see, touch, or even look at a credential without proper authorization, signed in triplicate.

With those assurances, I was hired as secretary to the director of the Democratic National Convention. While I worked on the convention, I was actually employed by the Democratic National Committee (DNC), and before I finished working there, I became executive secretary, administrative secretary, administrative assistant, and assistant to the director, and if we could have thought of any other titles even more powerful, I could have had them too, but I couldn't have a pay raise; the DNC had no money.

Wealth is a mighty force at any time. In politics wealth has awesome influence. While the absence of money can be, and is, a hindrance to a political party, it always has the promise of once again being in power and flush with cash. Hence it is never good to slight a future powerhouse.

The Republicans were in power with President Nixon running for reelection. So most of the cash went to his party. But we had credit.

A friend and I were discussing an upcoming Democratic Party event to be held in Washington. She casually mentioned that we had for several years owed a big tab at the Mayflower Hotel so we had better hold our event there. When I challenged that premise, she replied that since they had been nice enough to wait to be paid, the least we could do is to continue to give them our business, on the cuff. One day, sooner or later, we would be able to pay all our bills. Apparently, the Mayflower agreed, because that's where we held our event.

Frustrated at our budget limitations, I asked Bob Strauss, who was then treasurer of the DNC and its future chairman, why we had our offices in the expensive Watergate office building when we could save money by being in lesser offices. He explained that money is attracted by money and a show of wealth is important. Wealthy donors want the reassurance of dealing with successful people/organizations, which is why in politics wealthy donors give to both sides; it's an insurance policy. So, while we did not have the cash flow we needed, it was very important to keep up appearances.

Our funds may have been low, but the perks weren't too bad. The convention was to be held in Miami Beach, Florida, in July of 1972. Six months prior to the convention, we began traveling back and forth to Miami every week. We had three days in Washington, three days in Miami Beach, and a half day of traveling each way. Dick had a DNC credit card so we always ate well—very well.

At each of the hotels in which we would be placing delegations, we were given complimentary rooms and, since they all wanted the wealthier delegations to be placed with them, they often included a little wining and dining; perhaps a basket of fruit and occasionally a bottle of wine. The wealthier local contributors took us sailing for the day on their million-dollar yachts or entertained us at parties or dinners in their homes. Certain kinds of bribery were apparently okay. And of course money was seeking power.

Shortly before the convention, when available rooms were practically nonexistent and press credentials were equally challenging to acquire, a reporter friend sought my help, asking what it would take to get both. As we were walking to the car that evening, I made the mistake of telling Dick about the request, saying, "I told him I could be bought."

Dick stopped dead in his tracks and, with a startled voice, said, "You said what?"

"I said I could be bought—it's the price that's in question," I laughed. Then I realized how concerned Dick was, so I hastily assured him, "Don't worry, I've already taken care of it."

His shoulders sagged as he resumed walking. Shaking his head, he mumbled, "Don't scare me like that."

What Dick didn't understand was that finding my price has never been easy.

Finding My Price

Our offices in DC were in the Watergate office building, across the street from the Howard Johnson motel, where I parked my car. Next door to the Watergate is the Kennedy Center, which has a wonderful upscale restaurant where I occasionally was fortunate enough to dine.

One particular day stands out in my memory. Early in my tenure at the DNC, a gentleman who I had recently met and had lunch with a couple of times took me to the Kennedy Center for a delightful lunch. The room was much brighter than the other restaurants in which we had previously dined. And while we discussed the joys of horse racing, the thrill of watching your own horse as it noses out the competition, and speculated on his horse's chances in its next race, I noticed what I thought was a slender wedding ring, tucked behind a large college class ring on his left hand. Now maybe it was a wedding ring and maybe it wasn't a ring at all, after all men don't usually wear *two* rings, but I blurted out to him, "Are you married?"

He assured me he was and continued on with his description of the horse race. After lunch as we walked back to my office, with his limousine following slowly behind, he suggested I fly with him to Paris that weekend on the new Concorde. We could see his horse run at

Longchamp, have a few days in Paris, and be back in time for work on Monday. While I pondered that picture, he suggested with a wave of his hand that he would just love to fix me up with a nice place of my own in one of the apartment buildings nearby where we could have more privacy for our lunches. A vivid image of those very intimate lunches flashed through my mind as we walked. When we reached the elevator to my offices I paused, gave him a regretful smile, and said, "I'm sorry, but that's just not my cup of tea." I never saw him again.

Amazingly, that same evening I had a date with Daniel, whom I had known since just before I went to work on the Hill. He was a wealthy Bolivian from Cochabamba, and we had gone out off and on for years. He also took me to the Kennedy Center for dinner, to the very same table where I had lunch, where the very same waiter served us, with a very discreet, raised eyebrow just for me. And there on the table was a gift from Daniel of two beautiful unset topaz stones he had brought me from his most recent trip to Brazil. What a day!

I had met Daniel in a drugstore while I was sitting at a counter having a Coke and studying for my class. Since I was about to vacation for a week in Puerto Rico, I wanted to speak to the natives in their own language, so I was taking Spanish at the Berlitz School of Languages. When Daniel said he was from Cochabamba, Bolivia, the picturesque town we had flown to after building those outhouses, it was like old home week.

We always dined at the best restaurants and then would go somewhere dancing. He loved to dance. Early in the evening I could understand him, but as the night wore on, not only did his accent seem to get thicker but, as the music got louder, his voice became softer. Certainly, I had more difficulty hearing him. I found myself sitting across the table from him not understanding a word he said but smiling and nodding in agreement. Periodically I'd stop him and ask, "What did you say?" just to be certain I wasn't agreeing to some outlandish thing.

While I always enjoyed myself with him, I wasn't romantically interested in him, so I usually put him off when he would call for a date. But he was persistent; therefore, our dates were usually a month or six weeks apart.

With that scenario it was probably another six weeks before we went to dinner again. As usual, we started with champagne and caviar, my favorite. Over drinks he told me that he had recently acquired a gold mine as payment for some legal work he had done for a client. It was still early in the evening so I'm pretty sure he said the mine was so lucrative that they were simply picking up four to five ounces of gold from the ground daily. Or was it forty-five ounces of gold daily? And they hadn't brought in the big equipment yet.

In any case, I tried to calculate how much that was at the current price of gold. Unfortunately, I needed both hands for my calculations and he was holding one of them. Then with a small frown he said they had run into a problem. I stopped counting and asked what the trouble was. He said with a twinkle, "We've just discovered oil on the gold mine." Hello!

The only picture I had of what a gold mine should look like came from old western movies with a prospector walking out of a mine shaft with his trusty burro at his side. Somehow this picture was not computing with what he was saying.

"How large is this gold mine?" I asked. He paused for a moment and then tried to explain. The land had been originally given to his client's ancestors by Ferdinand, the king of Spain, as a land grant that stated it included all the land that was visible from the top of a certain mountain, which he named.

"How much land do you think that might include?" I asked.

He paused again, thought about it and asked, "Well, how large do you think the eastern shore of Maryland is? Probably something like that."

The problem was there were some Bolivian regulations that were impeding further exploration of the oil fields. However, he thought he would be able to work something out since the president of Bolivia was his former college roommate.

Now we were talking. I thought I had found my price! When we went dancing that evening he seemed to talk louder too. When he mentioned he was going to the opening of a new restaurant the next week, one that had had a great deal of advance publicity, I was happy to agree that that would be wonderful.

All week I looked forward to our date. On Saturday as I began dressing, I also began to have a few misgivings. Daniel usually called to reconfirm our dates, and he had not done so that day. I couldn't not get dressed in case I was wrong, but as I reviewed our conversation of the previous week, I became more and more convinced he had not actually asked me to join him, which would have been logical on his part since I always put him off for a month or so. As I sat in my apartment all dressed up with nowhere to go, I began to laugh at myself. Strange how money can skew a picture! Of course, I didn't hear from him again for months.

A political convention is a huge event. Not many cities are large enough to handle either party convention. The Democratic Convention may have been much larger than the Republican one, but Republicans were the ones with all the money. We were running ours on a shoestring. No matter how many flags we might have at any given function, the Republicans always seemed to have more than we. This time we were determined to change the image. We hung a *huge* American flag in the hall, and in the end, we couldn't even afford to remove it, so we left it for the Republicans to use and to remove after their convention at the same site. Alas, at our convention the cameras didn't seem to show the flag very often, but at the Republican convention, the view of our flag seemed to dominate their event.

Our office, the Democratic National Convention, managed the operations of the convention while Larry O'Brien, chairman of the Democratic National Committee, oversaw the political aspects of the Democratic Party. As the convention neared, I knew less and less about the candidates and more and more about the number of chairs in the convention center and why one shade of red carpet was better than another shade.

As we held organizing committee meetings with different groups, we should have had verbatim transcripts made of these meetings. Since we couldn't afford to hire a court reporter to transcribe the meetings, it fell to me, with my shorthand, to take the minutes. Obviously, the committee was in deeper trouble than they realized.

Once again, a one-eyed man in the land of the blind is king. At one point we interviewed maybe fifteen people to alternate the travel to Miami with me; and while there were many women with political experience who would otherwise have been qualified for the position, none of them had shorthand skills. I was all we had. That suited me fine.

What Goes Around, Comes Around

I believe each of us throughout our lives is either ascending or descending the ladders of life. We have them everywhere: in our social lives, our business lives, sports lives, whatever we do. Whether ascending or descending, after the event we leave others with a certain feeling about our actions—one of distaste, of appreciation, or of indifference.

As we ascend the ladder of success, therefore, it is important to treat those one passes with respect and consideration because at some point in our lives, we may pass them on our fall from favor. Or to put it another way, one never knows who may be guarding the gate one needs to enter, so be nice to all the people along the way—even if, for some reason known only to you, you want to smash them in the face as you pass them by.

Case in point: Viacom was a relatively new, but obviously growing, company at the time of our convention. For some time, they had been asking for floor credentials as they planned to make a documentary about the conventions, and it was necessary to have access to the action there. Because of the '68 convention's problems with fraudulent credentials, we were obsessed with who was allowed on the floor, so we had been very slow in giving a response to their several requests. Finally, however, we had agreed to meet with them to hear their petition in person and to make a decision, which would essentially determine whether they could attend the convention.

Because this was an important meeting for them, as is often done in Washington, the Viacom representatives brought with them someone who could help to influence our decision. In this case it was a political insider. No big deal—except it was Ted, my old love from my early days in Washington. The same Ted who had introduced me to the world of politics.

As I reached the reception area and went to the waiting Viacom people, there sat Ted. If I hadn't been looking at him directly, perhaps

I would have missed those flickers of recognition. There were two, actually. The first was one of recognition that it was I. The second was the realization that I was a gatekeeper, and he was in a lot of trouble.

I had met Ted the first summer I arrived in Washington. He was my first love, and he broke my heart. He was from Anniston, Alabama, and he worked for the Johnson administration as a political appointee at the Department of Housing and Urban Development. At the time he was assigned to President Johnson's reelection campaign.

I was twenty-three and in love. We would wander around Georgetown hand-in-hand planning our lives together. He even survived the kiss-of-death trip home to meet Mother and Dad. One autumn week after the election, Ted traveled with the president to Texas, and when he returned, he told me he had nearly picked out a ring for me there but decided we should choose it together.

Perhaps I had been naïve when he said he loved me and wanted us to marry, but I certainly believed him. Therefore, I was dumbfounded when one winter evening he walked into the house, stood in my living room, and out of the blue told me he had decided he wanted to position himself to run for the Alabama Senate and felt he would be a stronger candidate running as a bachelor rather than married to me, a northerner. What! I'd always thought I was a southerner, albeit at the northern fringes, but still below the Mason-Dixon Line. And with that, he turned and walked out of my life. No amount of weeping or agonizing could change his mind because he never returned my calls.

Now perhaps he had simply tired of our relationship, or perhaps he had found someone else, but in my mind, he could have been a tad bit more sensitive and caring than he had been that evening. Particularly since it took me months and months to crawl out of the hell, he had plunged me into.

Obviously, life hadn't turned out as he had envisioned it the last time we spoke. Now he was knocking at our door, with a large request for his client.

I smiled and said, "Hello, Ted." (When a gatekeeper has the power, she can afford to be polite.) He stood, said hello, and introduced me to the Viacom people. Then we all went to Dick's office for our meeting.

I don't remember much about the pitch they made. What I do recall is Dick's question after they left.

He turned to me and said, "What do you think?"

And I replied without a moment's hesitation, "Hell, no."

He laughed and asked if he should dictate the letter of rejection or would I prefer to write it. I said it would be my pleasure to take care of it. I could only hope this was a really important deal for Ted.

People are right when they say, "Revenge is sweet," or "What goes around comes around." But as I write this now, and as I look back at the pain I endured at his rejection, I also can't help thinking: what a waste, he wasn't worth it.

Ted wasn't the only person from my past whom I heard from while working at the DNC. A friend, who I had difficulty visualizing even at that time, called me to say he had recently returned to work after having been hospitalized for a while. He said he was a manic-depressive and while working at the Peace Corps he had been in one of his phases. He was the person, he said, who leaked information to the *New York Times,* and he was sorry his actions had caused me to be fired. It was nice to have the mystery solved, but I had moved on with my life, so we chuckled over some shared experiences and then hung up. The unintended consequences of his actions had hugely affected my life, but I had been fortunate—I had had family and friends who had surrounded me with their love and support, and I had survived relatively unscathed. But I had learned from that brief tenure that no matter how innocent your actions may be, perception is critical in life. It hadn't been fair that I should be penalized for someone else's actions, but that's life. And because I had picked myself up and moved on, I was enjoying an even better chapter in my life.

Putting It All Together

As the convention date neared, we moved our office to a suite in the headquarters hotel, the Fontainebleau Hotel. The phone system was not complicated. We had two five-button telephones in my office. They were constantly lit with calls on hold because there were so few places to send incoming calls; usually they were for Dick, Ed, or me.

Sylvia Chase of CBS News stopped in, as many of the reporters did, and was impressed enough with our operation and the authority I wielded that she asked to interview me for her national radio program about women in positions of power, about my role in the management of the convention.

As I recall, the women's movement had yet to kick in full throttle, so women did not expect to see other women in positions of influence. As D-day approached, more volunteers arrived to work at the convention. One was the administrative assistant to, I think, Pennsylvania's Speaker of the House. He moved in seamlessly, being as politically in touch as he was. So when a young woman arrived at our makeshift reception area in the elevator foyer looking for a paid position, I asked him to handle her. He must have told her he would check to see if there were any openings and to come back the next day. For there she was, still looking for a position. I was free, so I went to tell her there were no openings, paid or otherwise. She didn't like that answer and insisted on talking to the gentleman from the previous day. I smiled and said I'd get him. He and I chuckled as I passed her over to him: "Obviously she thinks you have more clout than I." So my volunteer met with her again—in her eyes the man appearing to be the more important person.

Everyone wanted to be on the convention floor. But we were holding firm with our plan to severely limit who had *entrée*. As it happened, Ralph Abernathy and the SCLC were one of those groups seeking tickets and not getting any satisfaction. They were very persistent about checking in daily for floor passes so they could lobby the delegates. Well, with our obsession on credentials, that wasn't likely to happen. On the other hand, we weren't particularly forthcoming with them about our concerns, and thus we kept putting them off.

Finally, one day I heard the only other secretary we had in our office say as she once again handled one of their calls, "Well, let's face it. They're never going to give you tickets for the floor!" *Good grief!* That might have been true, but it certainly wasn't how, when, or who we wanted to give them the word!

The next day Ralph Abernathy, backed up by about twenty or so reporters and cameramen, stormed into our offices demanding to speak to the manager. Then everyone barged into his private office and listened to, watched, and recorded Ralph Abernathy's tirade against Dick and the Democratic Party and its reluctance to give them access to the delegates and his demand for passes to the floor. Obviously, he wasn't thinking he could get the credentials, for how could he and Dick seriously negotiate with each other with all those cameras in their faces? Eventually the confrontation was over, Ralph had made his point, and everyone left without Dick having said very much at all. Well, Ralph had his photo op. He certainly hadn't gotten his credentials, and now he never would.

As you can imagine, we worked closely with the network representatives as they set up their booths and prepared their people for gavel-to-gavel coverage. Each time there is a convention, one of the networks handles the liaison work for all the networks. They do this on a rotating basis. That year CBS had the lead and producer Fred Friendly was our contact. It was he and Edward R. Murrow who had taken on Joe McCarthy years before (Fred's role was depicted in the movie, *Good Night and Good Luck*). There was an obvious respect, even reverence, in the voices of the reporters, even Dick Murphy's, when they learned Fred Friendly was the liaison. He was extremely easy to work with, but not knowing him or his reputation, to me he was simply another member of the press, and I always delighted in the press corps.

Security was enormously important. Several items stand out in my memory related to security issues. For one thing, Dick Tuck's shadow loomed large over American politics and, as we would later learn, it affected both parties. Because of Dick's contribution to the chaos at the '68 convention, Dick Murphy was determined to distribute the credentials on a daily basis in order to minimize the possibility of forgery. This not only caused enormous headaches each day, but because the tickets had to be delivered to the thousands of people attending the convention, it ultimately tied our hands just at the moment we most needed flexibility.

Second, the Secret Service was a force to be dealt with. They had veto power over anything that might seem to compromise their protection of a candidate. Because of Robert Kennedy's assassination, each announced candidate for the nomination had Secret Service protection, and that year we had had eleven candidates. Even so, Governor Wallace had been shot and paralyzed earlier that year while campaigning in Maryland.

Clint Hill was our liaison with the Secret Service. It was he who had pushed Jackie Kennedy back into the car when the president was shot in Dallas.

Because Carol Welch had spoken of Clint so often (we had even spoken on the phone one evening when Carol and I were roommates), instead of feeling a sense of awe with Clint, I was relaxed. Thus, our working relationship quickly evolved into one of cordial respect. That was good because I came to rely on him during the convention.

And third, Dick Murphy had a security system installed in our Miami Beach office. Security systems were rare in those days and Ed Cubberly, the assistant manager, and I were puzzled as to why we should even have one. We often forgot to arm it at night and would simply shrug in the morning when Dick would admonish us once again about setting it. Why would anyone want to break into our offices? It was just a convention, and the Republicans were here shadowing us anyway.

President Nixon had wanted to have the Republican convention in California until a Republican Party scandal with International Telephone and Telegraph had forced them to cancel those plans at the last minute. The result was that the only possible place to hold their convention was Miami Beach because they could piggyback on the infrastructure we were already putting into place. So in the spirit of cooperation, the Republicans sat in on many of our organizational meetings!

Therefore, you can imagine our shock when Dick took Ed and me aside one Sunday morning in June to inform us that burglars had been caught breaking into our Watergate offices the night before. Larry O'Brien's phone had been tapped, along with another one in the office. Although Dick didn't know where the investigation would lead, the break-in seemed to point to the Republican Party. Obviously, it was important to be sure the security system was on each night. We never forgot after that.

We Could Plan, but We Couldn't Control

George McGovern was the expected nominee. Unlike the '68 convention, which had many states with unpledged delegates, "favorite sons" (usually the most powerful politicians in the state, who controlled the state's delegates' votes so they could wheel and deal at the convention for political favors in exchange for their support), or other strong contenders with a large block of votes, this time the nomination had been sewn up early by McGovern.

That was the good news. The bad news was because McGovern controlled so many delegates, he also controlled the rules of the convention. And one of the rules he implemented was that dissenting voices would be heard. Therefore, people holding minority positions on every issue involving the party's platform had an opportunity to speak. And that extended the hours of the convention to the breaking point.

Not only was the convention boring, but the big speakers—the keynote speakers and the party leaders—sometimes did not reach the microphones until after midnight. Both the Democratic and Republican conventions have a section of the best seats reserved for the party's fat-cat contributors. Too bad the Democratic Convention's was directly across from the network sky booths, because our fat cats rarely showed up. So a great big section of the hall was usually empty and it was always the one in the camera's eye. And because of our obsession about forgeries, we had no extra tickets to distribute to fill up the seats.

There seemed to be credentials for everything: press, delegate, alternate delegate, platform, guest, student, and maybe even candidates. My credential was the highest, the podium credential, which allowed me to go everywhere. Or it would have if I had ever been able to keep it. There were only seven of them printed for each day so I was always giving mine to someone else. I would take the next highest ticket I could lay my hands on and have Clint initial it so I could roam around. Each day it seemed that the credential he initialed was lower on the totem than the previous days; finally on the last day it was entirely blank. As he initialed that one, Clint quipped, "Lucky for you this is the last day; since you have sunk so low, tomorrow you wouldn't have gotten into the hall!"

Then he gave me some instructions. The first was that there would be no more friendships that day. When the candidate arrived, I was not to attempt to approach either him or Clint, period.

The second instruction was that if an emergency arose and they had to hustle McGovern out of the hall, they would (pointing to some double doors leading outside) be going through those doors. "Do not under any circumstances," he warned, "follow us through those doors. If you do, I'll kill you." That certainly caught my attention.

Late that evening, long after everyone in the civilized world had gone to bed (maybe around 1:30 in the morning), Ted Kennedy arrived at the convention. He was to introduce the nominee. I went out back to meet him and conduct him to one of the private rooms behind the stage. Approaching the senator, I noticed Dick Drayne at his side whispering my name and previous role in his life in his ear. It had, after all, been two years since I worked for him. I was relieved Dick had been there to tell him since I was confident the senator would have fumbled the ball otherwise. He couldn't remember names any better than I could.

Ted Kennedy's speech galvanized the people. McGovern's put them to sleep, but by then it seemed like it was nearly dawn—around three o'clock.

And then the convention was over, and with it my job. For the third time in two years, I was once again unemployed. Ogden Nash once said, "Home is where, if you go there, they have to take you in." So, home to Mother and Dad seemed the logical place to go—again.

The FBI Comes Calling

Not long after I had crashed and burned at home and caught up on my sleep, the phone rang. When I walked into the kitchen after answering it, Mother asked, "Who was that?"

"The FBI," I replied.

"No, you're kidding," she said in disbelief.

"No, I'm not. They want to talk to me about Watergate. An agent will be over here in about a half hour."

She looked at me with a very skeptical eye and pointed out, "It's not nice to fool your mother."

I assured her I wasn't fooling around. Well, she looked at me as if I was a stranger she had suddenly realized was masquerading as her daughter. But sure enough, not too much later there was a knock on the door and in walked FBI agent Dick Mayo. We sat in the den and talked while Mother hovered in the kitchen, trying to hear what was going on.

Most of his questions focused on the empty office at headquarters that had been designated for the liaison to the governors. But the position was never filled.

"Who used the office then?"

"We all did," I replied. "If you wanted to have a private conversation, or if a call came in as you were leaving, you ducked into that room to take it. Otherwise, it was pretty much vacant."

The burglars had been caught in Larry O'Brien's office trying to fix the wiretap on his phone because it wasn't working properly, but they had made no effort to remove the tap on a phone in a vacant office.

"Why then," he wanted to know "would the wiretap have been left on that phone?"

I had no ideas.

He left. Dad came home. Mother hurried to tell him the FBI had just been there to see me about Watergate. I think my status had gone up.

Later when I was at headquarters emptying my desk and visiting with friends, I got the juicy scuttlebutt.

"Did you ever use the phone in the vacant room?" someone asked.

"Sure, lots of times," I said.

"Well, apparently so did Beth. According to the FBI, who has listened to the tapes, she was having a scorching-hot affair with a senator and would use that phone to give her best friend a blow-by-blow account of her activities the night before. She was so graphic they could hardly believe what they heard. One agent said he sure would like to get a look at her!" We all laughed.

But there were other ramifications. The tapes were to be used in court against the burglars, but other people had also used the phone, some of whom had been setting up their own extramarital assignations. Those men were scrambling to keep the tapes out of court. Plus there were others who had said some things that could be highly embarrassing if publicized. Had I, my friendly informer asked, made any potentially embarrassing calls? Because, if so, a group of people was hiring an attorney to help them keep the tapes out of court. I assured her I was not concerned about any of my calls.

As I left the office, I ran into Beth sitting in the reception area. She said she had been at home in Missouri and had been called back to DC by the FBI.

Did I have any idea why they wanted to see her?

Thus ended my days in Washington.

Friends and family outside the Beltway scoffed at the third-rate burglary, as President Nixon's press secretary called it, even though I insisted there was something rotten in DC—something my friends and I couldn't put a finger on but that we knew existed.

Eventually during the Watergate hearings, testimony indicated that Nance Lyons, Mary Jo Kopechne's roommate, had indeed been under surveillance by the Plumbers, a group of black ops people working for the Committee to Re-elect the President (CREEP). In addition, Ted Kennedy's chief of staff Dave Burke's concern about undue surveillance and wiretaps in Hyannis Port during Senator Kennedy's Chappaquiddick ordeal were confirmed.

Dick Tuck's influence had longer tentacles with more serious consequences than one could have imagined. According to CREEP, the "dirty tricks" that their members were convicted of conducting against several Democratic candidates, and for which they ultimately served prison time, were a much heavier-handed effort to emulate Dick's tricks against Republican candidates.

It turned out that the personnel man who fired me from the Peace Corps, who had seemed to know so much about me, had at that time just come from the Justice Department, where he had worked for a man who was convicted as one of the Plumbers and sent to jail.

Testifying before one of the Congressional hearings, an official, when explaining his abuse of power, commented that the amount of influence he had had went to his head. He had forgotten that what power he had was not really his; it had derived from his boss, which in his case was the president of the United States. When one has the power, it is often difficult to remember that power corrupts, and total power corrupts totally.

I understood what he meant, for I had had a smaller taste of that power during my years on the Hill, and it was very heady stuff. I count myself fortunate that I had the wisdom to leave when I did, for had I continued I would not have liked the person I feared I was becoming: a hard, narrow-minded egotist.

Moving On

People often asked me after I left Washington if I missed it. I've discovered that I've been very fortunate because I have been able to turn a page to a new chapter in my life and have not looked back at the previous chapters, wishing I could relive them or do some things differently. Because I have tried to savor my life as I lived it, and because I knew when I was in Washington I was living history and paying attention to what was happening around me, I was generally ready to move on when the time came.

Of course, I also had a unique advantage because so many of my friends were in the media, either covering politics or participating in it, I felt I was still in touch with them as I watched their lives unfold:

- Dave Burke, EMK's chief of staff became president of ABC News.
- Dun Gifford, EMK's legislative assistant became my niece Robin's boss at Oldways Preservation and Exchange Trust, a non-profit, changing the way people eat, her first job after graduate school.
- Cassie Mackin, my roommate, became a political reporter for ABC until her death from cancer in the 1980s. She covered the conventions in '72.
- Jeff Greenfield, RFK's legislative assistant, became senior political consultant on CNN for years before moving to CBS.
- Terry Smith, from the *New York Times*, went on to Public Broadcasting Service and regularly appeared on, *The NewsHour with Jim Lehrer.*
- Dick Harwood's son, who looks just like him, is John Harwood of the *New York Times* and CNBC and regularly appears on TV.

And the many other reporters, columnists, and authors who populated my world in those days continued publishing, broadcasting, and reporting, so when I see them, and lately their children, on TV or see their names in print, I feel a connection that is still warm and friendly.

CHAPTER SEVEN

FRANK PERDUE: TOUGH MAN, TENDER CHICKENS

*Your schooling may be over, but remember
that your education still continues.*

—Anonymous

Out of work, collecting unemployment insurance, living at home with my parents, resigned to returning to Washington but looking for a job in Salisbury with no real expectations for a decent one, I stopped by an employment agency just because I had to do something to show I was trying. Because I commanded a much higher salary in DC than I could get in Salisbury, I barely made any effort to look for work. To be honest, I was tired of beginning new jobs, learning new routines, new faces, and new office politics. But one day the phone rang. The employment office had arranged an interview for me at Perdue, Inc. So I put on a nice professional outfit and went to check them out.

Terry Conway said at the beginning of the interview that the only reason he was even meeting with me was because he wanted to see what a "Loudell" looked like. All my life I had had mail addressed to me as

"Mr.," so I understood, laughed, and didn't take offense. The problem was he asked me back for a second interview, which was way too early for serious job possibilities since I hadn't finished my minivacation at government expense. At this interview he mentioned he had checked my references!

Trying to remember who I had used, I looked up and asked if any of them remembered me. He laughed and said the first person he called was Dick Murphy, who had immediately said, "Whatever you do, keep her away from numbers."

Terry looked at me and said, "You do know I am vice president of finance, don't you?"

"Well," I replied, "he's right. Every time he said one number, I seemed to hear another." Then I sat back and waited for the ax to fall. It didn't; instead I became the manager of the secretarial department. Terry had called it the clerical pool, which was such a demeaning description that I determined then and there that that image had to change quickly.

Working at Perdue was an eye-opener, literally. On Capitol Hill I had come into work at the civilized hour of 9:30 or 10:00 a.m.

In Atlanta, I arrived punctually at 9:00 and left promptly at 5:00.

Working on the Democratic Convention had been a twenty-hour-a-day ordeal at the end, but when I was in the Washington office, I had strolled in at 9:30 a.m.

Not at Perdue. Because the women in my department had to clock-in no later than 8:00 a.m., I arrived at least by 7:45 and often earlier than that. Sometimes, to my horror, it was dark when I reached the office, and occasionally I even heard a rooster crowing!

My first day at work, Terry took me aside and suggested that in order to show who was boss, I ought to fire someone. Hello. This certainly wasn't going to be a soft, easy-going place to work at all!

Before I could take aim at anyone, people began lining up to quit. The first day four women, for various reasons, gave notice. So much for showing who was boss. I was begging them to stay.

Frank Perdue, president and CEO of the company, liked to meet the new hires, so my first day I was summoned to meet with him. Frank was not a stranger to me, as I seemed to have known, or known about, him for most of my life. He'd been called Chick Perdue at the country club when I was a child, and I recalled that his wife, Madeline, had for years delivered baby chicks to the farmers in a converted school bus. Now this mom-and-pop shop had turned the poultry industry on its ear, shaken up Madison Avenue, put Salisbury on the map, and was able to demand and get a premium of ten cents a pound for its product.

Frank welcomed me to his office and, like the suave gentleman he had become, he offered me a seat, came around from behind his desk, sat in a chair across from me, and welcomed me to his company. Then he looked me square in the eye and declared in his high, squeaky voice, "I would never have hired you myself, but you're here now, so we'll see how you do."

"Why not?" I blurted out.

"Because it's been my experience that children of professional people, particularly doctors, don't feel they have to work very hard for a living, that they are basically lazy. Doctors don't work particularly hard themselves; they take the weekend off and then they take Wednesday or

Thursday off during the week. Which day does your father take off?"

"A half day on Thursday," I replied, dumbfounded. Who should I be defending here, Dad or me?

The conversation continued for a while longer, but when I left his office, I had no doubt that Perdue was going to be as tough to work for as everyone had warned.

When I moved home, I collected unemployment benefits and often had Marie, Mother's maid, sign my form. That evening as I drove Marie home, I told her I had found a job at Perdue. Marie reared back and shot me a look I'll never forget.

"Are you working on the line?" she asked. I hurriedly assured her I would not be plucking chickens with her friends. Obviously, she was relieved to hear that, as her shoulders relaxed and she settled back into the car seat. I would have hated to diminish her standing in the world by taking the wrong job.

Someone with a perverse sense of humor must have looked down from the heavens and laughed because the first report brought to me for my signature had not a single word on it, not one! It was all numbers. The form was obviously familiar to someone, for it didn't even have a title, but I thought it too ludicrous for me to sign it. Then other similar reports poured in. So I called everyone together and told them that in the future I wasn't signing off on the reports; they had done the work, they should stand behind it by putting their own names on them, not I. They seemed happy with my first decision, so we were off and running.

It wasn't long before Frank came to me with a project: find out what made his chickens so good. I gawked at him for a moment and exclaimed, "Don't *you* know?"

"No. I just know they are better than anyone else's. If we were suddenly to lose that edge, we might not be able to get it back if we don't know how we do it."

Thus, was launched my career as chief taste tester. First, I needed to learn something about taste testing, so I went to the General Mills organization to see their test kitchens and testing panel, then on to the University of Pennsylvania to check out their panel. I began cooking. Not one or two chickens, but dozens at a time. We had fifteen or sixteen categories to measure and record for each bird we prepared. I just love precision work; it dovetails so well with my tendency to BS my way around problems I have no answers for. At Perdue I discovered the importance of severely curtailing the BS. They lived by the numbers. I never found the secret ingredient, but when things needed testing, I was the one to turn to.

These days CEOs are frequently featured in advertisements. But in the early 1970s they were anonymous entities. Until, that is, Frank became the spokesperson for his chickens. He was such a natural, it's hard to believe now that there could have ever been any hesitation about using him as the spokesperson.

During my youth, Saturday morning radio was always ruined because all music stopped while the local chicken auctions were broadcast. It was a big step for Perdue to move from selling off his live chickens to processing them himself and then an even bigger step to ask for a ten cent per pound premium for them. When the distributors and grocers in the northeast refused to carry his product, Frank made history by going over their heads to the public and encouraging them to ask their butcher for his chickens by name.

In order to do this, he needed good advertising. And true to his nature he first researched thoroughly the subject of advertising. Then he went to New York and interviewed every advertising agency there.

Many of them laughed at him and his ideas. Some came up with ridiculous ideas like putting him in silly situations, such as holding flapping chickens under each arm while pitching his product.

Frank liked to tell the story about how he finally chose his advertising company. After hearing the ideas of all the advertising agencies in town, it was time to make his choice. He invited the account executives from a well-known agency to lunch (I can't remember which one, but maybe BBDO). Naturally thinking they had won the account, they descended en masse to the Plaza Hotel for lunch. As they sat down at the table, Frank told them right off that he had narrowed his list to three agencies, and they were not one of them, so he would be buying lunch. They went into the dumps but rallied after a couple of drinks.

What he wanted from them was advice on which agency to select. Eventually he went with Scali, McCabe, Sloves advertising agency and the slogan: "It takes a tough man to make a tender chicken."

With humorous advertising and a good product, Frank was wildly successful in appealing to the consumer to look for his golden chickens with his name on them. And so he successfully branded a heretofore unidentifiable commodity—chicken.

Working at Perdue was like taking a postgraduate course in business. Never having been around a businessman, I relished observing how a successful corporation outdistanced its competitors. Perdue had developed a seven-pound roaster by genetically altering its broilers and breeding them to have large breasts. In fact, the breasts became so large that the chickens' legs were too small to hold them up, so they had to develop roasters with bigger legs, too. The result was delicious as well as unique. I was surprised to learn other companies didn't have the genetic farms that Perdue had.

Thanks to Scali, McCabe, Sloves, Perdue chickens came with a recipe tag dangling from a wing. The new roaster required new recipes and I was the one to work with a nutritionist in New York who created them for us. I farmed out to friends the first few recipes she sent us. It wasn't difficult to get volunteers to cook a free roaster with our recipes and to then evaluate them for us.

Things had moved right along and by Christmas we were well launched. The nutritionist sent me a fruitcake that she had made from her own recipe, which was really very good. It arrived a little the worse for wear since the Dansk soufflé bowl she had prepared it in had broken along the way. There it sat on my desk when Frank stopped by. Before he left the office he paused in the doorway, eyeballed the open package, and observed that company policy dictated that employees were not allowed to accept gifts from any vendors and I should actually return the fruitcake.

I looked him hard in the eye and laughed as I said, "Do you really think I can be bought with a fruitcake?" He paused, returned the look in the eye, smiled, and replied, "I guess not. Besides, she sent me one too, and I'm not sending mine back either." Then he strode out of the office.

While sitting in my office doing some paperwork about a year or so into my career with Perdue, Frank stormed in, sat down, and said in his feisty, high-pitched voice, "Have you seen the *Boston Globe* today?"

Of course I hadn't. "No," I said very carefully. "Why?"

"There's a full page ad in it saying Buddy Boy is going to take me on in Boston and intends to whip my ass. I was going to let Esham have Boston, but not now!"

Otis Esham and Frank had grown up together. They both had poultry processing plants, and were practically neighbors competing with each other. Frank's ad campaign had been so successful that at the time Perdue chickens had a 97 percent recognition factor in New York City. He himself had become a celebrity. But Frank's competitive nature could not tolerate the kind of challenge Otis Esham had issued, and so he took him on. And defeated him. Put him out of business. Bankrupted him. The only thing the Eshams were able to salvage from the bankruptcy was the family farm, which they went on to develop as Nithsdale, one of Salisbury's most upscale subdivisions.

One day Frank called and said, "I know how interested you are in politics and I have to attend a fund-raiser at Rogers Morton's in Easton. (Morton was our Republican congressman, brother of Senator Thurston Morton, whose office had been next to mine on the Hill.) Would I like to go with him? Of course I would.

Well, it was an eye-opener. I had attended a number of local political gatherings, but here were some entirely new faces, people I hadn't even been aware were so politically active. Then I woke up to the fact that these were Republican Salisburians I was seeing, not Democrats. It was an entirely different group of people, of course. I felt like a mole in the enemy camp—although the truth of it was that I liked Rogers Morton and always voted for him.

On the way home, Frank saw a silo operation along the road and wanted to know more about it, as he might be interested in buying it. So he pulled into the plant and talked at great length to the night watchman. The next day he dictated a lengthy memo to himself about the conversation and then called to alert me that he'd dictated it for transcription by one of my secretaries and would I please be sure it was kept confidential. Naturally I read it very thoroughly before delivering it to him.

"If you buy that operation, I imagine the night watchman can count on a job with you," I said, as I handed him the memo.

"Not at all." Frank looked me dead in the eye and said, "He'll be the first to go."

"No!" I exclaimed. "Why would you fire him? He's been so helpful to you."

"That's the problem. If he would spill his guts to me, he'd spill them to someone else. I would never take that kind of chance. Suppose he told my competitor what he told me!"

Then he amplified his statement by explaining, "I have an obligation to the employees of this company. They have invested their futures in my dreams. I have an obligation to them, as management, to keep my company solvent. If I were to employ someone who could jeopardize my company, it would jeopardize everyone's position. Management's greatest responsibility to its employees is to stay healthy, to stay in business."

This, I knew, was a Republican businessman's manifesto. Over the years I've brought it out and examined it again and again. Wherever I have worked since then, I have first examined management's attitude about its business. It's enabled me to be much more tolerant of management decisions that at first glance seemed less than generous to its employees.

Frank's advertising slogan, "It takes a tough man to make a tender chicken" and his humorous ads about his chickens' breasts and legs had made his name recognition in New York so phenomenal that once he ran an ad showing just the back of his head. The caption read,

"Quick, name a chicken." So when I went back to Katharine Gibbs for a management seminar, everyone was eager to hear how Frank really ran his business. We were a small enough group of women that we could sit in a circle and discuss various ways to handle issues. It didn't take long for everyone to become horrified—and to wait in anticipation for my responses, which of course I relished.

To begin with, they couldn't believe Frank's personal secretary was on the time clock. I assured them that not only was she on the clock, but so were all the other secretaries and that if anyone was late three times in a month—and one minute late counted as lateness—then that person was excused from work for a day without pay. Of course, they had to keep up with their work, which meant they worked late for the balance of the week to catch up with their reports. I think I did that once early in my tenure, and it was so painful I never did it again. But the threat was still there.

Each night the salesmen on the road would call into the office and dictate their reports, which a transcriber would type the next morning and give directly to Frank. It was a demanding position requiring good typing skills, and it was difficult to keep filled because of Frank's frequent demands. Because I had been concerned about having no African Americans in my department, I was delighted to hire one who had worked at UMES and could type like a whiz. Unfortunately, she couldn't spell worth a darn, and there were no automatic spell-checks in those days.

After two weeks of rewrites on every one of her reports because of so many spelling errors, I let her go. Let me say here that firing someone is not easy. At least for me it was always traumatizing. I hated it. Maybe because I knew what it was like being on the other side? When I told the people at the seminar I had fired someone after two weeks, they were flabbergasted. They assured me they couldn't even dream of something like that. And when I assured them she went quietly because we both knew she couldn't do the work, they were dumbfounded. Apparently, no one went quietly in New York.

For New Yorkers, Perdue's image of phenomenal success must have translated into an image of uptown sophistication. So naturally I had to straighten out that misconception. Frank's father, Mr. Arthur, the founder of the business, was in his mid to late eighties and worked at the office as the mail boy. He would shuffle around the office delivering the mail and zero in on you with his one good eye if he thought for half a second that someone had used inappropriate postage for any mailer. He drove the largest Mercedes Benz Frank could find for him in the hopes its strong body would protect him, should he end up in an accident.

We could always tell when Mr. Arthur arrived at work because he would bump the side of the building when he parked and the building, being wood frame with an old, working silo attached, would shudder. When MBAs would come from New York to interview for a position, they were always astounded by the quality of the corporate headquarters. I would tease them about it, because I knew what they were thinking.

"A little surprising, isn't it?" I'd ask when I was meeting with them. They would look around at the building that looked as if it could burst into flames at any minute, nod their heads, and say, "I thought it would be better than this."

My office was an interior one with no windows. Occasionally I would think about what to do if the building caught fire but reassured myself that, with the overhead sprinklers, I would be able to get out should a fire occur. I mentioned that to Terry one time and he looked around and asked, "What sprinklers?"

I pointed up and said, "Those."

He laughed and said, "Those aren't sprinklers, they're smoke detectors. They'll just let us know if you are burning. They sure won't put the fire out," and walked away, chuckling.

Later when Terry suggested building a new corporate headquarters, Frank nixed it, saying, "How will that generate income? We'll stay as we are." Which we did for a number of years thereafter.

Frank believed in management by fear. He felt that if an employee wasn't scared he might lose his job, then he, Frank, wasn't doing his own job well. He was doing just fine. I didn't know any employee who felt secure in his position.

That said, Frank also welcomed and encouraged innovation. If you thought you had a better way of doing something, you were invited to try it. So when the secretary who handled customer complaints observed that people might be overcooking the broilers and roasters, thus making them tough, she and I did some test cooking. And indeed, we did show that our cooking instructions, which were the industry norm, were wrong. The chickens should be cooked five minutes per pound less. When we took our findings to Frank, he declared that if an independent tester agreed, he would change his recipes. They did, and he did.

It was a small detail, but Frank was obsessive about details. It was his strength.

Frank's way of showing "your business is important to us" was by answering the phone promptly. Perdue's standard, for example, was that the switchboard phone should never ring more than four times before being answered. If it did and it was Frank on the line, he routinely asked for me instead of whoever he was calling. Then he reamed me out because the receptionist hadn't answered quickly enough. It didn't matter that she was handling twelve hundred calls a day, if the phone rang five times, the customer might hang up and call a competitor.

On Saturdays the switchboard was open until noon, and then calls were switched over to the hatchery where whoever was on duty there could pick them up. One weekend a friend called Frank at the office and commented that he was surprised to find him there because no one had answered the phone earlier. At Frank's exclamation, the friend said, "You should try calling yourself sometime."

When Frank hung up he did indeed call himself and was horrified to realize the phone was ringing and ringing with no one answering. Laying the receiver on his desk with the phone continuing to ring, he raced downstairs, jumped into his car, drove over to the hatchery, which was down the road and around the corner from his office, and stormed into the building where the phone was still ringing. When Frank confronted the person in the hatchery, the man explained that when he was running certain equipment, such as he was doing then, he couldn't hear the phone. Frank acknowledged he was correct and said he'd have that remedied by Monday, which he did. He had a horn put on the phone that could have woken the dead.

Frank's, and therefore the company's, attention to detail was not confined to the operation of the office. One day while talking to one of the veterinarians, I exclaimed in frustration, "You have reports on so many things, I bet you even know how many times a chicken blinks!"

He looked at me for a moment while pondering my statement and then assured me they did not know that. However, he remarked, "We do know how many times in a minute a chicken pecks another chicken."

I was stunned.

"No kidding, how could you possibly know that?"

"Well," he said with a straight face, "we have someone sitting in the chicken pens at the research farm counting how often a chicken pecks its neighbor."

"Good lord, why?"

He explained they did it so they could test various environments to learn if more or less humidity caused excessive pecking or if more or less light affected them, and so forth. Obviously the more detailed information one has when making a decision, the better decision one can make.

I've tried to remember that during my real estate career. My customers seem much more comfortable with their decisions when I make the extra effort to seek out just that extra bit of information for them.

The first couple of years at Perdue seemed like a perpetual interview. It wasn't easy finding people who could do the work and do it under pressure. Frank would call me after he met with the new hires to give me his opinion. He was always abrupt with his calls and these times were no exception.

He began with "Well, she's not going to work out."

"Why not?" I asked through gritted teeth.

"I know her family and they're all lazy."

And sure enough I eventually had to admit she wasn't working out.

Another time he called and said, "You have a problem in your department. So-and-so isn't carrying her weight."

"How do you know?"

"Just watch her and make your own decisions, but I'm telling you there's a problem."

Sure enough she was cutting corners, not being as thorough with her reports as she should be.

Frank didn't miss much.

Eventually I got my department squared away and working well when once again someone gave notice. This time it was the person who answered consumer complaints. She had been doing a really good job, but now she wanted to fill a position that was opening up. I agreed, if she would help me find her replacement.

Consumer letters were important and Frank kept a close eye on them. So when I told him the current person handling the consumer letters wanted to move to a new position, and that I had a new person starting Monday, he went ballistic.

"I don't want any changes. The one we have answering letters is doing a fine job." With eyes blazing and his hands on his hips, he ordered, "Cancel the new hire! She doesn't know a *goddamn* thing about my chickens!"

Well, I too got riled up and said more than a prudent person should. Standing up and staring him in the eye, I responded, "I've seen her work, and she will be just as good. And she can jolly well learn what she needs to know about your *goddamn* chickens!"

Then there was a horrified silence as we glared at each other.

He warned me. "All right, if you think that much of her, go ahead and let her start Monday. But I want to meet her, and then we'll make the decision." And he strode out of my office.

"Fine," I said to his retreating back. And then I breathed a little easier. I had a trump card still to play.

Frank had a reputation for having an eye for women. And when I sent that beautiful young woman upstairs to meet him on Monday, I sat back and waited for his call. It came. "She'll do."

When I interviewed for my job, Terry had checked my references and Dick Murphy had been quick to say, "Keep her away from numbers!" I was always grateful for that cautionary advice because Terry had no illusions about my mathematical ability. In fact, he would chuckle when he saw me struggling with my taste-testing reports.

Therefore, when it was time to prepare the annual departmental budget, he sent Ed Ross, an accounting department manager, to help me figure things out. Together Ed and I came up with my budget, and I turned it in to Terry. Several weeks later Terry called me to his office to review and defend my proposed budget.

As he went through each line of the budget, I explained why it was important to have this particular increase for supplies or that increase for salaries and so forth. I was doing quite well until he got to the bottom of the page. Then he looked up with an incredulous expression and exclaimed, "This isn't even your budget, Loudell. It's another departments. You don't know your own numbers, do you?"

Well, of course I didn't.

So, he gave me my budget and told me to review it and get back to him.

It was much more difficult the second time around; after all, I'd used up my best explanations on the wrong numbers!

I may not have worked at the processing plant, but I got to know a number of the people working there. Some of the line people were on my taste-testing panel. The cook would call me whenever she was serving muskrat because she knew I liked it so much, and I would sit and eat with the other folks, discussing the finer nuances of good muskrat.

In addition, Perdue sponsored some line people to take a Dale Carnegie course at the same time I took the course, so I got to know them as well.

Frank had asked me to join him for a meeting at the processing plant. When we walked into the building, a number of big, black linemen were taking a break and simply hanging out around the entrance. We walked through the gauntlet they created. Spying one of the men from the class, I spoke to him, he said hi back to me, and then we sealed the greeting with a high five. Frank looked at me and said with wonder in his voice, "You're one of the few people I know who is as comfortable talking to a lineman as to the president of the United States." It was one of the nicest compliments I ever received.

We are each of us responsible for our own lives. The directions we take are determined by the choices we make. Mother used to say, 'If you don't know what to do, do nothing." But doing nothing is also a choice.

The Women's Rights Movement hit its stride in the late '60s and early '70s. Suddenly, large corporations were sensitive to the absence of women executives in their ranks. With my resume and contacts, I felt confident I could have been recruited to be a vice president of some corporation. All I needed were a few business courses, probably not even a degree in business; just some basic knowledge would have been helpful.

I chose not to take that path. Some people might say I was lazy, and I probably wouldn't argue with them. But I think mostly I didn't want the corporate politics.

I was probably the only female manager at Perdue; at least I was in the corporate headquarters building, that smallish wooden building with a working silo. So I was pleased when one day I was invited to join the guys at a local roadside watering hole just up the road from work. It was a small bar with a number of pickup trucks parked in front. Inside was clean and bright with a bar and a single shuffleboard machine. One of the guys bought me a beer and explained that the managers sometimes got together for a beer or two on their way home. A couple of them were already playing shuffleboard on the machine (it was like a bowling game, and the object was to "knock down" the ten pins by sliding a puck under them). The winner played all comers and as long as he won, he could continue to play.

It was enjoyable standing around sipping a beer, watching the game and being included in the fraternity I had just discovered existed. Finally, everyone had played and they turned to me and asked if I'd like to give it a try.

"Sure, I would love to try," I said with a smile.

There followed some instructions on how to do it: Don't shove the puck too hard, 'cause it goes fast; you get two tries just like in bowling; there are some nuances to moving the puck around, but you'll pick them up as you learn it; just relax and try it a little. Then they all stood back and watched.

It was a lovely machine. I almost caressed it as I reached for the puck. It seemed like an old friend for it looked exactly like the one I used to spend hours playing at the country club in my youth. Muscle memory kicked in as I slid the puck down the board and hit a strike. A small cheer erupted from the men for beginner's luck. And then after a few more practice slides, I said I was ready.

Then one after another I beat them all! This was fun. I had another beer, thanked them for including me, and then headed for home. I was never invited back. *Oh, damn. Was I supposed to lose?*

Early in 1976, I sent a memo to Frank and Terry saying that it was time to break up my department. When I first started there, the department was little more than a "steno pool." Now the women were true assistants, and I felt they should be located nearer to their immediate bosses and not in a bullpen with a supervisor. In short, the department had evolved to the point where it was no longer needed. That suggestion was rejected by both Frank and Terry. My department would remain.

But it was time for me to leave, so once again God sent a messenger. First, it was Joanna Abercrombie, a childhood friend and college roommate, asking if I would be interested in taking the real estate course with her.

Even after passing the course, I was reluctant to leave the security of a regular paycheck. Bill Ahtes was the most prominent real estate broker in town, so I interviewed him. I couldn't begin to consider real estate, I told him, if I couldn't earn at least $12,000 a year. He thought about it for a while, nodded his head, and said, "Yes, that is possible." Still, I hesitated. So then came the kick in the butt. This time Terry was the messenger.

He fired me. Terry called me back to the office from vacation to have a meeting one July afternoon. While I was off, Terry had called a meeting of my department. He asked them to evaluate me. When the responses were not to his liking, according to some friends who were managers of other departments and for whom those women worked, he exerted a little pressure and then left them in the conference room for a couple of hours to discuss it among themselves in order to come up with another answer. They weren't stupid. They decided I was not a good manager. Terry was "shocked," after all he had thought all along, I had been doing a good job! But the girls had voted; they wanted me out of there.

Gosh, here I had been working for a dictatorship that governed by fear only to discover that during my vacation the winds of democracy had blown through the office, and I hadn't been there for the vote.

When I asked him what this was all about, Terry finally admitted that Madeline Perdue had come to see him. She had been told by some mutual friends of ours that they had seen me with Frank in Jamaica, and she wanted me fired. When I told Terry I had never been to Jamaica, with or without Frank, he leaned back in his chair and said, "Well, what can we do now?"

"Well, I cannot go back to that department after they voted me out, that's for sure," I sobbed.

Then I hit the ceiling of my own unpreparedness.

"There's no place else in the company for you," he sighed. And I couldn't argue that point.

So we agreed that I would leave—but I asked for and received a three-month severance package.

That was on a Friday, the traditional day for firings at Perdue. I was cleaning out my desk on Sunday evening when Frank walked in and sat down. He said he was sorry to hear I was leaving. I told him what had happened from my perspective, since he already knew Terry's. He leaned back in his chair and thought for a moment and then replied, "Well, yes, I was with a tall blonde woman in Jamaica and I did see [our mutual friends] there. I can see where from a distance they might have thought she was you." End of discussion. End of Perdue.

Once again, I was huddling in a corner feeling sorry for myself. Only this time I was in my brand-new condominium, on which I had yet to make my first mortgage payment. After licking my wounds for a couple of weeks, I called Bill Ahtes and began my real estate career.

CHAPTER EIGHT

REAL ESTATE IS DEFINITELY NOT BORING

The difference between a job and a career is the difference between forty and sixty hours a week.
—Robert Frost

When I began in real estate in September of 1976 there was no sales training, the listing contract was one page, the sales contract was two sides of a legal sheet of paper, a hundred-thousand-dollar buyer was something to get excited about, and a million dollars of production annually was very good. Now the contract of sale can be fifty to sixty pages long and the listing contract thirty-five or more pages, and you're starving if you do only a million in sales.

Two things have not changed, however. Everyone who comes into real estate says they enjoy working with people, and they want flexible working hours.

Not long ago a friend told me her daughter was thinking of trying real estate. She would be graduating from college soon and she already knew she didn't like early morning hours, so the idea of "flexible time" in real estate had a great deal of appeal. What did I think?

Real Estate Is Definitely Not Boring

With tongue in cheek, I assured her that the only time there is in real estate is "flexible time." Her daughter wouldn't have to come in early, except, of course, for the weekly sales meetings, or floor duty that often begins at 8:30 in the morning or training classes that start at 9:00. A recent out-of-town meeting required leaving the office at 6 a.m.

Having worked "a real job" for so long (that's one where you work forty hours during the week with weekends off), I find it difficult to take much time off during the week without guilt. Of course, most buyers are also working those hours, so if you aren't working on the weekends, you are probably not making ends meet because that's when the buyers are available to look

If you are fortunate enough to have buyers, they often can't see property until after work, say 4:30 or 5:00, or on weekends. After spending a half day finding appropriate houses and setting up appointments for showings, you can wait and wait for them, but they may never call to say their plans have changed, or they'll call a half hour late to say they're just crossing the Bay Bridge and how much farther is it anyway? That's when flexibility really kicks in.

"Flexible time" means evening appointments to list houses or to present contracts after the kids are down for the night, say around 8:00 p.m. These appointments usually run a couple of hours.

All this evening work leaves the daytime hours free to "market" real estate, follow up on whether anyone is doing what they said in their contracts that they would do, find vendors to do the inspections, or sit at the house while the inspector takes two or three or four hours to check everything out. (This is excellent on-the-job training for learning more than you ever wanted to know about high nitrates in the water, roofs leaks, foundations cracking, wiring, plumbing, termites, wood borers, fungus, and lest we forget, the ever-popular septic systems.)

And of course, Sunday open houses are the epitome of "flexible hours" because one can choose whether to give up the whole day and have back-to-back open houses or simply take two or three hours from the middle of your afternoon to sit in someone else's house and be bored. You do this for two reasons: One, the sellers want you to do it. Two, you might actually find a customer. Selling the house that day is such a remote possibility that it doesn't even enter into your calculations.

All of which translates into "flexible hours," which means working seven days a week.

Then there is the danger. From 1982 to 2000 there were two hundred Realtors in the United States who were murdered by their customers, as a police officer pointed out at a sales meeting on protecting ourselves, a female

Realtor not only advertises with her photograph, she then adds her home phone number plus the address where she will be sitting in an open house all by herself. When he said, "Don't do that," we all laughed and said, "Of course we will do that. It's how we make a living."

Over the years I've taken self-defense courses, martial arts classes, and listened to others give advice on keeping oneself safe while showing property. I do try to practice some precautions. I rarely go upstairs with customers in an open house, even if I know them, because while I'm upstairs how do I know someone else hasn't come in downstairs and hidden away? I try always to have everyone go ahead of me into a room, up the stairs, or through a door, whether he's my brother, a friend, or a stranger. That's not just to unblock the "Wow!" factor of their seeing a room for the first time, it's also designed to put a predator in front of me rather than behind me. Of course, I'm not perfect with that, but it reminds me to be careful. Naturally I don't expect my brother or my friends to attack me, but if I develop the habit, perhaps it will save me

Real Estate Is Definitely Not Boring

sometime when I really need it.

Since I began my career in real estate, it has changed its face so many times that just thinking back on my early career amuses me. Take door knocking. Bill Ahtes encouraged me to go into an area, any area, after the kids were off to school and the mother had had her chance to sit down and have her morning cup of coffee. "Just knock on the door and ask if she is thinking of buying or selling a home," he advised.

I would sit in my car and look down a quiet street where I was confident no one knew me, for I sure didn't want anyone to recognize me going door to door like a vacuum cleaner salesman! I would sit there trying to talk myself into getting out of the car and actually knocking on a door. Eventually after about twenty minutes or so, I would give up and drive off, declaring, "This street doesn't look ready for me." No problem nowadays. Today we don't even consider doing that. If you didn't get shot for trespassing, it's probably because there was no one at home.

However, one cold autumn day I knocked on one of my parents' friends' doors and asked the woman if she knew of anyone who wanted to sell her house. She pulled me into the house and fussed over me. "Oh, Loudell, that is such a difficult thing you are doing, knocking on doors. I am just fixing lunch for Dick, who will be home any minute. You must stay for lunch." When her husband came home, she went into overdrive about how difficult it was, doing what I was doing, knocking on doors looking for business. In the end they listed a building lot with me for $10,000, which I sold for $8,000. I'm pretty sure that was my only success at door knocking, and I'm positive I never did it again.

Then there were cold calls. I took a course that encouraged me to sit and call everyone in the reverse directory phonebook. The reverse directory phonebook shows the home phone numbers for everyone on a given street. I would sit and call fifty to a hundred people looking for just three appointments. Oh, what a joy that was. Now, we have that wonderful "do not call" list. Gee whiz, can't make those calls anymore.

Both of those activities ranked right up there with root canals. Frankly, I don't know how I survived so many years in the business. Having said all that, I can't think of anything I'd rather be doing.

Today a new agent gets so much training, his head must spin. I could have used some when I began. It took a while to get a first customer, but finally someone from Perdue agreed to look at houses with me. And then, be still my heart, she said she would like to buy the house. I had no idea what to do! Quickly I hustled her over to Johnny and Sammy's restaurant for a cup of coffee while I called the office. Help! What do I do now? There was no manager there (I've discovered over the years they are never there if you really need them), so John Robinson, an experienced agent, said he would help me.

He asked so many personal questions of my customer, I was horrified. Questions such as, "How much does your husband earn? How much do you want to put down? What kind of debts do you have and for how much? How long has your husband been working at Perdue? How good is your credit?" She was as upset as I was. She left to get her husband.

The husband was one of Terry's MBAs, so I relaxed a little because I knew he'd know the numbers, which he did. We wrote an offer; the counter offer was higher than he wanted so I had him sit down with Bill Ahtes. Bill explained that the difference in what he offered and what the seller wanted amounted to about thirty dollars a month in additional mortgage payments, which was only one dollar a day more, and once the tax benefits were realized, he could hardly afford to not buy the house. I must have missed something in this presentation because my friend/customer stormed out of the office declaring that Bill had just tried to swindle him and that at the moment he was thinking of suing me, but once he cooled down perhaps he would reconsider. Scratch one friendship.

Things settled down after that wobbly beginning. Having flung myself into my work, I've actually survived without any broken bones, although I've had a number of sprained ankles and skinned hands and knees as I've fallen off front stoops and down broken steps, stepped into hidden holes, slipped on icy stairs, and inadvertently jumped into a slimy ditch. I've stepped into a hornets' nest and been stung thirty-eight times by the swarm, been knee deep in mud, and plunged headfirst down a whole flight of stairs. Good thing I'm a natural athlete!

Over the years, I've made beds, washed dirty dishes, walked dogs, and cleaned up the poop of those that should have been walked. I've stumbled into bedrooms with couples in bed, shown wrong houses, ignored used condoms lying on the floor, and set off innumerable security alarms—all of which have helped me hone my diplomatic skills.

I had gotten my sea legs and was feeling much more comfortable in real estate when a friend, Bernie McCurdy, asked me to help her out. She was going away for the weekend and her out-of-town buyers were to be in town then. If she would set up the itinerary and appointments, would I take her customers out? Of course I would.

So Saturday morning the couple and I headed out to look at houses. The first one was on West Hampton Circle, not far away. When I knocked on the door, the wife opened it and the loudly barking dog let us know he was there too.

The woman said, "Let me put the dog out back, and I'll be right with you."

As she took the barking dog outside, I replied as I always do, "Don't worry, we'll just look around, and if we have any questions, I'll be sure to find you." I guess she didn't hear me.

It was a small house with a living room/dining room combination and there sat the husband having breakfast. *Really, couldn't they have waited until after the showing?* Well, I talked to the customers about the nice space and suggested they check out the kitchen while I spoke to the man of the house. Trying to be friendly, I remarked that breakfast looked good, and he said it was. Through the window I could see his wife was having a little difficulty with the dog, so we moved on. I directed the buyers to the bedroom section, which was three bedrooms and a bath, so it didn't take us long to see the whole house. By the time we finished, the wife had also finished. We met again at the door.

She said, "You do know that Ahtes and Hanna doesn't have our house listed,"

With a confident smile, I bluffed. "Well, maybe not with our company, but it's in the MLS [Multiple Listing Service], so even though you've listed it with another company, I can still show it."

"No, no, we haven't listed it with anyone. It's not for sale," she insisted.

"Well, this is 312 West Hampton Circle, isn't it?"

"Yes, it's 312, but it's *East* not West Hampton Circle. You need to go further around the circle. The house you are looking for is over there," as she politely pointed us in the right direction.

Oh.

So we trooped out of the house and continued around the circle to the correct house, which had a for-sale sign on it, a big clue.

Trying to turn lemon juice into lemonade and at the same time wipe egg off my face, as the three of us stood in 312 *West* Hampton Circle, I waved my hands and said, "Wasn't that fortunate? Now you have a house to compare this one to."

"Yeah, we prefer the other one," they said morosely. Well, that was a good start.

We continued on our way and saw several more listings, one of which they liked and ultimately wrote a contract on.

The next weekend, I was showing my cousin and his wife houses in an upscale neighborhood, and after looking at several, we headed to the last one I had planned to show them. It was a For Sale By Owner home. As we drove to the house, I told Grason about my mishap the previous weekend and he, his wife, and I had a good chuckle.

There were only two houses on this particular block, and as I had asked the owner to do when I spoke to him on the phone, he had removed his for-sale sign. Unfortunately, both houses looked pretty much the same, having been built with the same color brick and being about the same size. I was just beginning to wish I had written the house number down when Grason said, "We don't need to see this house; we've already decided we want the last one we looked at."

"Great. However, they are expecting you, so let me just run up there and let them know we aren't going to look at it." Then I jumped out of the car and walked to the house. When the woman answered the door, I explained the situation.

She said, "Loudell, you have the wrong house. You want the one next door." *Damn!*

So I walked across the yard, knocked on the other door, delivered my message, and returned to the car. It was rocking. As I opened the door Grason and Bebee were hugging their sides as they howled with laughter. "Let me guess," Grason said, "you were going to show *us* the wrong house too!"

Well, these things happen. I just wish they didn't happen to me so often.

When a friend called from the hospital and asked if I could help her new hire find a place to rent, I said of course, even though there would be no commission involved. I made a few phone calls and was ready to go when she arrived on Saturday.

She didn't like anything. So I called my broker's secretary at home and asked if she knew if the broker had any other rentals I could show. Yes, there was a townhouse that had just become available. She didn't have the key, but the tenants were out of town for the weekend and usually left the back door unlocked. She gave me the address.

We went over, looked at it from the outside, and walked around behind to check the door, which was ajar. It was an attractive place. I dropped my card on the counter and we headed for the second floor. When we reached it, the bedroom door was open and there lay the couple in bed! Asleep, thank heavens!

We tiptoed down the stairs, picked up my card, and hightailed it out of there.

She liked it. So I wrote up the lease and left it and the deposit on the secretary's desk. Monday, Betty called me and said, "Did I say apartment B? I meant A. You must have shown the wrong place. But they're all just alike, so if your customer is okay with it, I'll just switch it to A."

I called the renter, and she said that would be fine.

I love politics, so I was helping Ted Venetoulis in his campaign for governor of Maryland. As the tricounty chair for the lower shore, I had a meeting with the candidate and a few other people at my apartment the same Saturday the tenant was due to move in. My phone rang and she hit me between the eyes. "These houses are nothing alike. The other house had a bow window, this doesn't, it isn't as clean, and furthermore, this and that are wrong. And if you don't believe me, the couple in unit B is home and we can go ask them to show you!"

Good grief! That scenario was too awful to contemplate. I could visualize at some point her telling the couple about our little mistake when we found them in bed. Ordering her not to say another word, I said I would be there in ten minutes; I turned to my gubernatorial candidate and said, "Carry on; I have a little crisis I need to take care of. I'll be back shortly." *I hope.*

And God was smiling on me that day, for on the short drive to meet the customer I passed another townhouse complex with a rental sign. And when I knocked on the office door the manager said her tenant had moved out during the night, so she had a unit available. I grabbed my tenant, directed her moving truck to follow us, and took her to her new digs. And returned to my meeting, all within a half hour.

An Intervention

It may have been the mid-1970s, but for a woman to remain unmarried was a whispering offense. I guess Mother and Dad were hearing things or simply feeling alarmed for me. Old Maid was a term still in use then—although my sister-in-law dressed it up a bit as she would sometimes jokingly call me the Maiden Aunt.

One evening Mother and Dad asked me to come over for a drink. As I sat there in the den they expressed their concern that I wasn't married yet. What had I been doing? Certainly, it wasn't from a lack of dates, so there must be something *I* was doing wrong. Good heavens, what was this? An intervention on getting married?

Mother asked, "Loudell, do you ask your dates questions about themselves? Men like to see that a woman is interested in them."

Dad asked, "You don't talk too much do you? Men don't like women who talk about themselves too much."

"Politics. What about politics? Men really don't want to talk to women about politics."

"Are you sweet and nice to them? I hope you show them your sweet side, because men want a wife who is sweet and nice."

And so it went.

At twenty-five I was working on the Hill. There was too much going on then to be distracted with marriage. At twenty-seven, there was Robert Kennedy's campaign. At thirty, it would have worked. I was being fired from the Peace Corps and it would have been nice to have a wedding to plan. Alas, no marriageable men were around. Here I was at thirty-five and most of the "good men" had been taken.

When I was fresh out of college, I wasn't so concerned what a man's job was—he could have been a ditchdigger then, as long as he had prospects. But by thirty-five, my expectations were higher. He needed to own the ditchdigging company—or be on his way to owning it.

As our biological clocks ticked louder and louder, I watched friends panic. One got pregnant, married, had a wonderful child. And then became bored and unhappy. Another married an abusive man. Meanwhile other friends were whispering in my ear, "I wish I'd done what you did, waited to marry."

It wasn't as if I didn't have opportunities. Lord knows over the years my sister-in-law tried hard enough to fix me up with a number of marriageable men. One was a cardiologist who I rejected and who ultimately married and moved to Texas. His wife shot *him* in the heart.

Another was someone she had met at an open house party she attended at some friends' house. That was a fun blind date. As we arrived at Phil and Jacquie's Ocean City home, I reassured him that this would be enjoyable because the only other people there would be our mutual friends, the Reeves. That's when he turned to me and confessed, he had crashed the party where he met Jacquie. At about the same time, Jacquie was telling the Reeves who was coming to dinner! After that strained evening, he must have wanted to make it up to me because when we got to my apartment, he came in with me. I left the room for a moment and by the time I returned he had used the opportunity to take off all his clothes. He was obviously quite proud of his family jewels, which I can attest were impressive! He was way too fast for me. Couldn't he at least have kissed me first!?

Perhaps I *was* a little too liberated. There was one guy I had been dating. He loved sports, having played football and baseball in school. Our dates usually had something athletic involved, whether it was bike riding or playing tennis... well, the tennis was unfortunate.

Salisbury has some fine public tennis courts in the city park, and as a teenager that was where I hung out. You could usually pick up a game there as Bill Riordan, Jimmy Connor's manager who lived in Salisbury, was often on the courts and would give a little impromptu lesson if one asked. Usually there were plenty of people playing tennis.

However, when my date and I were there, we had the courts pretty much to ourselves. We began hitting the ball back and forth to each other. It didn't take long to realize this was not his game. When I asked if he'd played before, he grinned and replied, "No, but how difficult can it be?"

That was fine. We could just hit some balls and have an easy time of it. But no, the competitor in him wanted to play a set. I hesitated. "Why don't we just hit some balls? There's no need for a game."

"What's the matter? Afraid I'll beat you?" he taunted.

"No, let's just hit the ball some." I equivocated.

"Come on, Loudell. Let's play a set. If you're worried, I'll spot you a game or two."

I gritted my teeth and countered. "That won't be necessary. Let's play."

It wasn't difficult to win the first couple of games. The problem was that the more he lost, the more he seemed to ridicule my play. Well, there's only so much a person can take, and apparently my bar was quite low. Concluding that he and I really were not so compatible after all, I began placing the ball a little more carefully... just outside his reach... and then I jammed it in close to his feet. In all, I was really on my game, and of course he had no game. *Damn*, there was just no way I could be the little helpless woman.

Even so there had been times when I had been close to getting married. But it seemed I could never synchronize my efforts with the men I was serious about. If he was ready to marry, I wasn't. If I was ready, he wasn't. Bottom line, here I sat with my parents and their little inquisition.

At the time, I was standing on the cusp of a new era, thanks to the Women's Liberation Movement to which I'd given so little attention. As Bob Dylan sang, "The Times They Are a-Changin'" and I was the fortunate recipient of good timing. It was becoming socially acceptable for women to have a career. If they chose to, they could have it all: a career, marriage, and children. Or in my case, a career. And what better one than that in which I found myself—real estate.

So having the intervention with my parents was helpful because it forced me to make an assessment of my situation. If I was going to marry, it was time to do it. If not, it was time to get serious about a career. I decided that if I wasn't swept off my feet in love, I wasn't getting married. Life was too good as it was to be messed up with a marriage just for the sake of being married. And as much as I would have enjoyed having children, it wasn't necessary for me to have a child to "feel like a woman." The birth of Phil and Jacquie's son, Phil, III, seemed to signal the end of birthing for our family, for it sure took the pressure off me to produce a son!

So, while I assured Mother and Dad, I would be much more careful how I conducted myself on my dates, I wasn't particularly hopeful—and neither were they.

CHAPTER NINE

OUTWARD BOUND—HAVE I LOST MY MIND?

Never give in, never give in, never, never, never, never...
—Winston Churchill

I'm not certain what sparked my interest in having a wilderness survival experience for three weeks in Big Bend National Park in Texas. Maybe it was some residual effects of having worked for Robert Kennedy. Maybe I thought I should know how to survive a hardship, test myself. In any case, when I told Mother and Dad, some months after their little intervention, that I planned to attend Outward Bound Survival School, Dad was horrified and Mom was enthusiastic.

Naturally, I had to get into shape. I turned to my trusty compatriot, Jacquie, and together we walked/jogged around our subdivision in the dark at six in the morning so no one could see us. At first, we could barely jog to the telephone pole just beyond her house. Eventually we were jogging almost around the one-mile circle. Without her help, I would probably have died or at least wimped out on my trip.

At the time, I was on the board of directors of the chamber of commerce, so there were plenty of people checking with me to see if I'd lost my mind. I assured them I had not. Sad to say, there were not many votes of confidence in my getting through this. Joanna Abercrombie's last words to me were, "Whatever you do, don't come back early. If you have to quit, go to Mexico, California, anywhere, but don't come home early!"

On New Year's Eve I flew to El Paso, Texas, took a train to Arlington, spent the night in a motel, and then joined thirteen others in the waiting room of the Arlington railroad station. There wasn't much conversation. One man was older than I, Spence, maybe fifty-two years old, everyone else appeared to be younger, much younger.

Right on the dot, the instructors came bounding into the station. They were so bright-eyed and bushy-tailed, with sunburned cheeks of red, it was enough to make you ill!

They drove us to a nondescript place on the side of the highway. We jogged about a half mile or so down a ravine to where they had stashed some supplies. Then they divided us into teams, told us to lay out the supplies we had brought with us for Scott, the leader, to check out. We didn't have much: one change of underwear, one pair of shorts, a pair of long pants, a top, a wool sweater, and two pairs of socks. Soap and toothpaste were optional.

We stood in a line with our things on the ground in front of us. About halfway down the line, one girl had placed a soft, pure-white roll of toilet paper on top of her things. Every one of us kept one eye on it and the other on Scott as he worked his way along. I was prepared to use leaves on the trip, but I figured if she got to keep it, she would become a near, dear friend of mine. Finally, Scott reached the toilet paper. He stood looking at it and, shaking his head, solemnly declared, "No, out here we use smooth, appropriately shaped stones."

"*Stones?* What about leaves?"

He just smiled tolerantly and explained, "Loudell, all the leaves out here either crumble in your hands or have prickers. It'll have to be stones."

This was going to be rougher than I had thought.

Next we divided up the supplies into the backpacks they gave us and trudged back to the vehicles. Then they drove our team a few miles to another drop spot. Everyone put their packs on, picked their way down to the ground, and disappeared.

I, on the other hand, stood by the truck, looking around trying to figure how I was going to get off the elevated road and down to the ground. The road's foundation was built up so that it was about six feet up from the base. And they wanted me to pick my way over these big, loose road stones, which would have been perfect for a rock garden. With the pack on my back I was so off-kilter, I was concerned I would fall. Fear, however, can also be a motivator, and as I watched my team disappearing around the bend, I finally picked my way very carefully down the rock pile.

The first thing I discovered was that the pack pushed my head forward and down so I could easily look for those smooth, appropriately shaped stones. The second thing was that the pack was really heavy. (A jug of water weighed about eight pounds and we each carried two. Somehow, I ended up with a number of cans of food, which meant I was probably carrying about fifty-some pounds.)

Then I fell.

Carl, the second instructor, was strolling along just ahead of me when he heard my body hit the ground with a whap. He came back to check on me. I quickly realized there was no way I was going to be able to get up with the pack on my back, so I reached out for a friendly hand up.

He crossed his arms, leaned against a boulder, and watched me.

I had a dilemma. I was afraid to take the pack off because I didn't think I'd ever get it back on without help, and Carl wasn't looking particularly helpful. But I definitely wasn't optimistic about my chances of just getting up.

I struggled some more, trying to get from a kneeling position to a standing position with nothing to lean on or cling to. It was hopeless. So then I very cleverly rolled onto my back and swung my arms to leverage myself up. Nothing moved but my arms. I tried again, still nothing. I was like a turtle on its back kicking its arms and legs to no avail. Poor turtle. Carl looked on. I couldn't even turn over. It was as if the pack were glued to the ground. Finally, waving my arms and legs a little more frantically, I said very sheepishly, "I need help."

Carl was flabbergasted. He stood up, shook his head, and finally, stretching out his hand, said, "You really can't get up, can you?"

"No!"

So he pulled me up. And off we went again. It was only a short distance to the camp site, maybe a mile. But when we got there it wasn't at my eye level. I looked around for everyone, and then Carl silently pointed up.

"What? Where?"

"We're camping up there in case there's a flash flood."

Now "up there" wasn't very high, maybe fifteen or twenty feet. I tried, but there was no way I could do it with the pack on my back. So Carl reluctantly agreed to carry my pack, and I climbed up the incline and crawled into camp on my hands and knees. It was not a good beginning.

It got worse.

Everyone was setting up camp, and I jumped in to do what I could to help. I certainly wanted to get into the spirit of the occasion. Scott taught us how to tie knots so we could create a lean-to for ourselves with our tarps. Next we learned to make a campfire from stuff lying on the ground. At least we had matches.

Then Scott and Carl went over to their own little campsite and left us alone to fend for ourselves over dinner. We really didn't know what to do. But we tried. To get a pot of water to boil over a campfire takes a long time, in case you don't know. And since a watched pot never boils and there were seven of us watching it, you can imagine how long it took! So we learned right then to get the fire started and the water boiling first thing when we set up camp. A hot drink tastes really good at the end of the day.

Then came dinner. We had a skillet but didn't know what to cook. We ended up having quesadillas made of raw onion, raw green pepper, and cheese cooked in about a half inch of oil. It was not good. Carl and Scott looked like they were enjoying their dinners. Later Scott suggested rather dryly that next time we might want to *cook* the vegetables before assembling the quesadillas.

And then we made a damn friendship circle and sat around telling people who we were, what we did, and why we were there. It was déjà vu all over again!

Except for Spence, everyone else was much younger than I. The next closest to my age was Scott, who was ten years younger. The youngest fellow was sixteen.

Eventually they turned to me. I told them I was a Realtor, thirty-six years old, and I was sure I had a good reason for being here. I just couldn't think what it was. Certainly, enough friends had asked me why I would want to do this, and I knew I had had a reasonable explanation for them, but for the life of me I couldn't remember what it was. I'd have to get back to them on that.

At last, it was time to sleep. I took off my boots and crawled into my sleeping bag under my tarp. No face washing, no tooth brushing, no clothing removal, and no lying awake either. End of day one.

Thanks to my walking/jogging training and to the others' lack of toning up for this ordeal, the second day wasn't too bad. At least I kept up. I fell lots of times and had to be picked up, but at the end of the day I overheard Scott telling Carl I was one of the first into camp.

Based on that, he chose me to be leader the next day. The leader picks the trails, reads the map, decides when to stop and eat, etc. That was not the time I should have picked to begin my diet.

I had decided the day before that if I had nothing else to show for this effort, I would at least lose some weight. So, on day three I skipped breakfast. By ten o'clock I was nearly fainting. Everyone had to stop while Scott figured out what was wrong with me. When I explained about the diet, he rolled his eyes, got out some peanuts, and made me eat several handfuls while everyone else hovered over me, watching.

Eventually we carried on; I led from the rear. We stopped early that day.

When I had been choosing which Outward Bound school I would attend, the choice was obvious. It was either cross-country snow skiing or this one course called "Deserts and Canyons." I hate being cold, so Texas and walking on flat land seemed perfect.

Well, in order to have a canyon there must be walls. And some of these walls have very large boulders that fall off them and pile up on the canyon floor. Since our canyons seemed to be narrow ravines, it was not unusual to have a pile of boulders obstructing the walkway. Then someone would call out, "Boulder problem ahead!" They seemed pleased. I wasn't.

One or two boulder problems would have been enough. But several each day, at least during the first week, was overkill. We had to climb over them. I don't do climbing very well. I had already established that fact in getting from the road to the ground. The good news was it was usually impossible to climb with the packs on our backs, so at least I could take it off and let someone else hand it up to Joe, our only knowledgeable team member. (He must have been an Eagle Scout in a former life.)

To get to the top of a thirty-foot rock pile meant choosing very carefully where you stepped. But it also entailed a lot of crawling and clinging. Ideally, one would simply reach for the boulder, place one's foot on it and leverage oneself up. Not me. I reached for the boulder, clung to it, brought my knee up, and, leaning heavily on both elbow and knee, pulled myself up. Then, of course, there was the next one, and the next, and the next. And then there was the descent. For me there was a lot of squatting and dangling of legs and hanging on for dear life, but I managed to not break anything.

Around the fourth day, Scott called us all together and gave us some first-aid lessons. He started out by saying, "Imagine Loudell has fallen again and she's unconscious. What do you do?" The consensus was that we would find the instructors, who often left us on our own with only a destination to aim for. And they would call in a helicopter to airlift the unfortunate victim to a hospital. It seemed likely that the victim would be either Spence or me.

Once again, Scott shook his head, no. There was no helicopter. Instead, he listed the steps to take: 1) determine what the damage is—broken leg, concussion, etc., 2) mark on the map the location of the victim, 3) two people hike to the nearest highway, which was many miles away, 4) flag down a passing motorist and hitch a ride to the nearest phone booth, 5) borrow a quarter from the Good Samaritan who picked you up, 6) call Outward Bound Headquarters in Santa Fe, New Mexico, to give them the information, 7) headquarters would, in turn, contact the roving instructor who would be patrolling in a jeep somewhere near Big Bend National Park, and 8) the instructor would, in turn, hike in with a litter, meet up with Scott and Carl, and come find the group, who was hopefully keeping the victim warm. Then they would carry said victim out of the park on the litter.

Looking at Spence, who suddenly seemed even older than he was, someone asked, "What if the victim's heart stops beating? Do we give CPR?"

"No."

Oh, dear.

The next day, Spence became too ill to go on. He had a terrible flu bug that he thought he might have picked up on the plane coming out there. Sure enough walking out was the only choice. Carl accompanied

Spence out of the park. He was too weak to carry his pack, so Carl carried both packs. I was impressed.

We continued on our trek. I tried to be really careful. Once again, however, I fell. As I knelt on the ground waiting for someone to come back and help me up, it gave me time to reflect on how often I had fallen. It was about the eighth time that day, and each day before I had fallen about ten times. It was getting very old.

Scott was with us at the time and as I was regaining my footing, I commented that I wished I had brought a cane or something. With that he walked over to what appeared to be a yucca plant, pulled out the stalk, and gave it to me.

"Here's your walking stick." It probably saved my neck. It became my most prized possession. To this day, I still have it.

Eventually the two teams rejoined for a day to learn some climbing and rappelling skills. Our team sat around our fire waiting for the water to boil for some hot tea. Scott and Carl were talking with the other team's instructors when Scott called for me to come over. When I reached them he said with a touch of awe in his voice, "Loudell, show these guys your bruises."

I rolled up my sleeves and pants. Both elbows and both knees looked as if they had been dipped into black ink. They were so bruised there wasn't even any purple, just deep, dark black. They were impressed, but there wasn't any sympathy. I went back to my group.

Being born under the sign of Leo, I have always enjoyed being in the spotlight. Frankly I prefer the take-charge role. But clearly I could not take charge now; I could barely hang on. It was a lovely discovery to learn one doesn't always have to be a leader. Sometimes being a follower is achievement enough.

A sort of pecking order had been established after my leadership day. While my walking and jogging at home had helped me to stay ahead of most of the team the first couple of days, once they found their pace, I found my place. It was in the rear. I may have been slow, but I didn't complain. Gradually a pattern emerged. While I always came in last, everyone at some point had a slow day, too, and would drop back to walk along with me for at least part of the time. After all, a group is only as fast as its slowest member.

At the end of each day, when we were all ready to pack it in, we usually had to make one final climb. The last time Outward Bound had been in Big Bend, which was about three years earlier, there had been a flash flood. People had died. So there was never any discussion about not sleeping above the canyon floor. The climb had to be done. Sometimes we were all so tired we could hardly move, but still we had to climb out of the canyon. Once, as I stood there looking up, pushed beyond what I thought I could endure and wondering if I was going to be able to make the climb this time, a team member came over to me and gave me a little pep talk.

"Come on now, I'll help you do it. I'll walk ahead of you, and you put your foot exactly where I have stepped. Together we'll reach the top." She led and I followed, literally in her footsteps. Totally focused on taking one step at a time, I managed to summon enough strength for just one more step until I reached the top.

Our reward? A gorgeous sunset greeted us when we reached camp. And that was when I learned a valuable lesson. The view from the top of your personal mountain is always beautiful. It doesn't matter if you climbed it alone or had help along the way. When you reach the top, the victory is yours and it is very sweet indeed.

In the middle of our three-week adventure, we had a "solo." In a solo, each student is placed at a particular spot and told to remain there, alone. He would have just a gallon of water to last through the solo, a tarp, his sleeping bag, and his journal. Our solo was three days long. There was no food. Foraging was not allowed in a state park, although there was nothing to forage for anyway.

I was in heaven. It was like having a minivacation in the middle of a vacation. I joked that, if I'd know there wasn't enough food, I would have paid more—but I really didn't care. To not have to walk, climb, fall, think, make a fire, or do anything at all, was more than I could have dared ask for. Thank you, God.

I set up my lean-to using my tarp. My knots were excellent. I laid my bed roll under the tarp, climbed in, and slept the next twenty hours.

Three days (well, now two) to do nothing, with no guilt. Have you ever wished for it? The next day I sunbathed in the nude, watched a hawk as he lazily circled overhead, wrote in my journal, and made major decisions, like where to piss and poop. That was it. I thought I was handling being alone very well—until I went to bed, that is.

I climbed into my sleeping bag and laid back, ready to go to sleep. But sleep wouldn't come. I tossed and turned for a while until I realized I wasn't comfortable. Moving my bag, I discovered I was lying on rocks. For twenty hours it had made no difference to me, but now that I was rested, I could feel each one of them, and they weren't comfortable. I moved my sleeping bag outside of the tarp, determined to sleep under the stars. That's when I realized the sun hadn't set yet. In fact, judging from its position in the sky, it was probably only 3:00 p.m. *Oops!*

When night finally came, I seemed to have slept all I really needed the day before, so I drifted in and out of sleep. It was lovely. The night was crystal clear and the stars overhead were huge—particularly the Big Dipper. It seemed to fill the entire sky as it silently glided across the heavens. Its stars were larger than ever and almost close enough to brush the earth. I felt as if this behemoth constellation was performing just for me as it gradually disappeared over the horizon and the sky began to show signs of the sun's imminent arrival. No wonder the ancients knew so much about the stars. That's all there was to watch at night, but what a show.

The next day was spent mostly sniffing my knife and hands. The night before our solo adventure, we had had a big dinner and I'd cut up the onions. Now the aroma of onions was all I had between me and starvation. I planned dinner parties. I created new dishes. I sniffed my hands. I grew hungrier.

Finally, Scott picked us up and we returned to camp, where a big pot of rice awaited us. We devoured it.

Apparently, we were on top of a huge mesa, near enough to the

Rio Grande that we could catch a glimpse of it in the distance. But now it was time to descend to the lower level. The tricky part was the fun part, too.

We would be working our way down a tight little gorge. Because this was a little more dangerous than anything we'd done to date, we were to wear our helmets. And while we were getting our helmets, we might want to pull out our bathing suits, too, and have them ready. *Uh-oh!*

We picked our way down a steep decline. Sometimes we had our feet on one wall and our butts on the other. Eventually we came to a tricky little drop. Several of the others ahead of me had negotiated the jump and now it was my turn. I sat on a boulder and looked over the edge, my feet dangling. Joe was there saying it was just a short little jump. All I had to do was land on the nice little boulder and stick to it. If I didn't stick the jump, I would continue to fall another five feet onto the nice, hard rock floor.

Picture sitting on the edge of the roof of a house and you have to land on the birdbath and stop. Unfortunately, there was no going back. Forward was the only choice. And, in this case, downward. So I jumped. I did hit the little boulder in passing. Good thing I was wearing my helmet because I had a very hard landing. I hit my head and banged up my knee, but nothing was broken and no one would have to carry me out. Which was lucky, because I don't know how they would have managed getting an injured person through the next rope problems. Just like a rock problem, a rope problem challenged us—in this case, climbing down the sides of the canyon while holding on to one.

We continued on a short distance to the end of the path where, standing elbow to elbow, we changed into our swimsuits. We were long past modesty. From there we were to rappel down a cliff face to the end of the rope, let go, and drop into an arroyo. After a short swim across the arroyo, someone would be at the other side to help us out. Nothing to it.

Scott turned to me, and only me, and asked if I could swim. I was indignant. I may be a klutz, but I'm a swimming klutz!

With a belay rope on for safety, and with Scott's instructions on rappelling ringing in my ears, I went over the side. Things were going pretty well, I thought, until my hand started hurting. What could be the matter? I looked at it and saw that my foot was on it. How in the world I could have done that I don't know. But it was quite obvious that nothing was going to happen until I pushed off with that foot, which meant grinding my foot into my right hand. Definitely an up-front and personal experience of being between the proverbial rock and a hard place. Of course, I did it, and my hand still has that scar to show for it.

Coming to the end of my rope, in more ways than one, I let go and dropped into the arroyo. Now, this water had never seen the light of day, and it was colder than hell. My head bobbed up and I started swimming. My intention had been to show off my beautiful swimming strokes from my synchronized swimming days in college, but with the weight of the helmet and tennis shoes dragging me down, suddenly just getting to the other side and out of the freezing water was all I could think of.

From there we went, in our cold, wet suits, to the next rope problem and rappelled again into another icy arroyo. The stress of the climb and the beastly cold swim left me trembling and in tears. The others weren't too much better. We huddled together for comfort while changing into dry clothes and then went to yet another rappelling site. We made camp not far away, which was good because my knee was already swelling up from where I had banged it up on the birdbath drop.

The night was cool and the hot food tasted delicious. We gathered around the cook fire trading stories about our solos and adventures on the ropes. After a while, though, I decided I'd better go to bed. I was so tired and aching, I couldn't keep my eyes open.

That's when I ran into a little problem. I couldn't figure out how to get up. It seemed as if every bone in my body was frozen in place. I put my hand down and leaned on it and nothing happened, so I placed it somewhere else and tried again, but nothing happened. Finally, moving very stiffly and using all my strength and every ounce of effort I had left in my body, I gradually rose to my feet. I teetered a little, but I was vertical. My walking stick, however, was down there on the ground. My gaze lingered on it in horror while I came to terms with the fact that I would have to stoop down on my worn-out legs to retrieve it. I glanced around the campfire and found all eyes on me. That's when I realized the conversation had faded away as everyone watched to see if I was going to make it to my feet.

"I think I'll go to bed," I explained with as much dignity as I could muster, "don't stop talking, you won't bother me." As I began to slowly and carefully lean down for my stick, Joe reached for it and silently handed it up to me. I was so grateful. Leaning heavily on it, I hobbled to my bedroll, shed my boots, crawled into bed, and was asleep before my head touched the ground.

The next day, what energy I had regenerated during solo seemed to have evaporated. I had no oomph. Joe watched as my sleeping bag refused to be stuffed into its little stuff bag. As I fought futilely to conquer this small task, he came over, took it from my hands, and with two efficient swipes at the stubborn thing, he had it put away.

It was a long day. My swollen knee had not improved overnight; even the pant leg brushing against it was painful. The blisters on my feet were killing me, my shin splints hurt, and my whole body was a mass of aches and pains. And there was nothing pretty about our environment. It looked like a moonscape, very desolate.

We were all feeling pretty bedraggled and I guess we must have been moving even more slowly than usual, because finally Joe, ever the leader, encouraged us to count out a cadence to keep ourselves going. As we approached the site of our new camp, where Scott and Carl were already set up and waiting for us, the final stretch may as well have been a hundred miles long. It should have been easy enough; after all, it was really just a short macadam road to a little car park area, but I'd run out of steam.

So I told them to go on ahead, I'd be along later, I just couldn't make it. That was when the whole team rallied around me. They slung their arms over each other's shoulders and created a long chorus line. And then together we did a little routine. Kick to the left, kick to the right, one step back, two steps forward, kick to the left, and so on, until we finally reached camp. The progress may have been slow, but the enthusiasm of the team boosted my energy level enough to propel me forward.

Scott came to my little pad to check on me. I was in tears once again seriously thinking that I could not continue, that I was slowing everyone down too much and that this could be the time for me to go home—well, not home, but to Mexico or California! The roving instructor was in camp, so if I wanted to leave, now would be the time to do it.

I was taking off my shoes and socks when Scott walked up and winced as he saw my feet. Going back to his pack, he returned with his first-aid kit and set to work on my blisters, which were bloody and seeping. He said if I wanted to quit, no one would blame me, but he hoped I wouldn't.

Tomorrow the two teams were to hike to Mule Ears and climb the peaks. But he felt I should remain in camp, soak my feet in the stream, and stay off them all day. If that didn't make a difference and I wanted to leave, I could do so then. His assertion that I wasn't ruining everyone else's experience reassured me. And with that bit of encouragement, I thanked him and told him not to worry; I would hang in there for the duration. I really didn't want to go to Mexico.

As the two teams left camp early the next morning, Scott made me feel needed by saying that because I was staying behind, there was no need for them to break camp. I was helping by staying behind.

The stream we were camping near was really small. It was quite shallow and one could probably have jumped over it. But it had running water in it. I crawled to the stream on my knees—why not? No one was there, so no need to put on a brave act. Even though the water was cold, it felt good on my blistered feet. While I was there, I filled a cooking pot with water and sponge-bathed myself. It was my first semblance of a bath in two weeks.

There was nothing much to do all day but rest and keep off my feet, which was exactly what I needed. The next day I was much better. It was good I had remained because the worst was past us. The hiking became easier and we all seemed to enjoy ourselves more.

We were coming to the end of our Outward Bound experience. There were just two more things to do. The last day there was a marathon, but before that we had a three-day trek ahead of us, called finals.

Scott gathered us together and explained that the two teams would come together one last time and then be redivided into three groups.

Each new group of four would consist of two members from my team and two from the other team. Each group would be given a map, compass, and food for their three-day trek.

The first group would consist of those the instructors thought were the strongest among us. They would have the most difficult terrain to cross; there would be no preset trail to follow; instead, they would simply bushwhack their way along.

The second group would have a more moderate level of terrain but would still be challenged. The third group, the slow one, would have the easiest route, which would be a well-marked path with cairns all along the way.

My hand shot up as I declared I would like to be in the slow group. Scott smiled his little smile and this time said, "Yes, Loudell, you'll definitely be in the slow group; the question is who will be in it with you!" I was content.

The next day the three groups went their separate ways while the leaders took their own path. While we had three days to reach our destination, each team had interim destinations it should hit each day for overnight camping. The instructors would check to see that we were there but would not come into camp. We were on our own.

Winter in Texas is not as warm as I had expected it to be. The sky was overcast, and with a little breeze, the weather turned raw. Right from the get-go, we were lost. So much for the clearly marked trail! We spent two hours searching for it, finally gave up and decided to wing it. Not a good thing for this group, I thought. The other girls were indeed slow, although I was in my traditional spot at the rear. We set our own pace, stopped when we wanted, and generally enjoyed ourselves.

That evening we set up camp, had dinner, and then felt our first drops of rain. Although it seemed to me, we were in a safe place, one of the girls was concerned about flash floods, so we moved our camp uphill in the dark. This time we didn't set our tarps up well, and when the rains began in earnest, we suffered.

What a joy it was to be lying under a very small, leaky tarp on the side of a hill in the dead of winter while the cold rain ran down the hill, over us, around us, and under us, no doubt on its way to becoming a flash flood somewhere.

Morning finally arrived and we managed a hot breakfast and took off. We had struggled with the map, never quite finding our path, but hoping that what we were on was an approximation of it. Our water was low, but thanks to the rains, we were able to fill our bottles from some standing puddles of rainwater. As we were taking a water break, we discovered that Pam had lost the map.

What the hell, it hadn't been that much help anyway. While we really didn't know where we were going, we had looked at it enough to know the direction was generally to the northeast. We still had our compass; we'd be fine.

It seemed to me we were either going up or down a defile (a narrow passageway) all morning. One boulder problem required us to pass our bags up, but it wasn't too bad. We stopped for lunch at noon, and at my suggestion, we spread out our wet sleeping bags with the hopes that a weak sun would dry them some. As we sat watching our bags dry, I took in the terrain.

All I could see were hills stacked up one after the other. In fact, the little childhood jingle began running through my head:

> *The bear went over the mountain,*
> *... To see what he could see*
> *... The other side of the mountain, Was all that he could see.*

It was so quiet I could hear three deer on a neighboring hill as they trotted on their way to who knew where. It was such a vast land, and we were such insignificant dots on it, I sure hoped we were somewhere near where we should be or we were going to be in deep trouble. We had not made our destination the previous night, so if we didn't show up tonight, the instructors would be out looking for us by tomorrow morning. Since we didn't know where we should be, I was pretty confident we wouldn't be where they would be looking. There sure were a lot of hills for them to look over.

The first week of our trek had actually been on a private ranch, Big Bend Ranch, which was four hundred thousand acres. Now we were in Big Bend National Park, which was much larger. It was beginning to feel even bigger as I contemplated being lost.

After lunch we resumed our hill climbing. It wasn't hard; it was simply tedious. Eventually we stopped for the night. One thing we had all agreed on, at my insistence, was that once we stopped for the evening, we would stay put until we were found. So once again the girls chose to camp on the side of a hill, probably because that was the spot where we all ran out of steam.

After setting up camp, two of the girls left to scout around, and Pam and I talked about our situation. Pointing out that we would have a much better chance of being found if we were on top of the hill rather than on one side of it, we moved our things to the crest. At our new campsite we displayed as much stuff as we could so we would be conspicuous to anyone on a nearby hill. My walking stick became a small flagpole.

Over dinner we discussed our chances of being found. On the plane ride to Texas, I had been reading the book *Alive,* which was about a rugby team that had survived a plane crash for more than ten weeks in the snowy Andes by cannibalizing their dead teammates and fellow passengers. I looked around, checking my food supply, wondering who I would eat first.

The next morning while we were having breakfast, we saw Bonnie, one of the instructors, walking over the crest of the hill next to us. We shouted and whistled and finally got her attention. Through purely dumb luck we were only a mile from where we should have been! And because we camped on the crest of the hill, we had been found. Bonnie left us her map and went on ahead. We packed up and, reassured that we were doing better than we thought, headed out. We had only seven miles to go; surely, we could make that without a mishap.

At lunch I discovered a Tylenol tablet in the first-aid kit. Oh, what a wonder drug that is! Throughout the three weeks I had obsessed about being so slow, but now that there was no real leader to say don't do it, I had been starting out ahead of the group, just so I wouldn't lag too far behind. Fortified with the Tylenol, I began walking faster. Now we're not talking Roadrunner here, but I was doing better. They in turn, being deep in conversation, began slowing down. One minute they were in sight, the next they weren't. One thing led to another, and before I knew it, I was alone.

I waited at the junction of two trails, but they didn't show up (not being a very patient person, I must confess I waited only fifteen or twenty minutes), and then I took off on the very well-trodden path heading for our final destination. It was the most enjoyable walk I had during the entire three weeks, so perhaps I forgot to remember the other girls. Anyway, I was happy, until I reached camp.

One of the first basic rules we learned when we started out was never, ever leave your group. Scott was not pleased to see me all alone. And he wasn't particularly impressed when I explained I had left messages and notes for the group all along the way. He jogged back to find the girls to let them know I was alive and in camp.

They straggled in that night around 10:30, and they were *not* happy campers. I couldn't blame them; if I had been them, I wouldn't have been happy with me either. But I wasn't them, so I rolled over and went back to sleep.

The next day, before the marathon, I watched Scott as he braced himself for a cat fight and called a meeting of our group. Tempers cooled down when I took full responsibility for leaving them. Actually, I got off pretty lightly, but they probably recognized that there was some culpability on their part, too, and were just as happy to not have to discuss it.

Then Scott advised against my doing the marathon because of my swollen knee. And with that, my Outward Bound adventure came to an end. Well, it was the end, except for cleaning up at the motel. I took three baths in rapid succession. When the water drained from the tub after my first bath, it left little eddies of dirt behind, miniature sandbars to show me just how dirty I really was. The water in the second bath was cleaner, so then I took a shower and washed my hair. That seemed reasonable, one bath for each week I hadn't bathed.

As I walked through the airport on my return trip home, I couldn't help noticing the glances from people as I passed them. Then I caught a glimpse of myself in some mirror and realized I was glowing, just like those instructors had been when they first walked into the train station three weeks before. I had challenged myself and triumphed. Pushing myself way beyond my personal limitations had not been easy, but that was what had made my victory so very special. I had persevered, and although it hadn't been pretty, I had succeeded, one step at a time. Outward Bound had been the most positive experience of my life. I was ready to take on the world.

CHAPTER TEN

BOCA RATON: A RARIFIED WORLD

Life is an adventure, dare it.
—Mother Teresa

Once again, I felt that guiding hand on my shoulder. This time it was a real estate salesman from Florida who walked into my office and asked me to help him sell some land in Pocomoke. On the drive there, about an hour away, he regaled me with tales of how easy real estate sales were in Florida. The more I heard, the more confident I felt that I could sell real estate in warm weather as easily as in cold weather.

That night I approached my parents and asked if I could live with them in their vacation condo in Pompano Beach while I established myself in real estate there. It shouldn't take long, maybe six months. They agreed. The next week I traveled to Florida, checked out the area, took a real estate licensing course, and found myself a broker. Then I came home, turned in my real estate license, and sold my condo.

During the 1980s I lived in Florida and sold real estate in Boca Raton, which was an eye-opener into how the other half (half, let's say 10 percent) live. While the Kennedys had money, they were very careful not to display it. Although their houses may have had extravagances inside, they appeared modest on the outside. They didn't drive flashy cars or wear showy jewelry.

The first week working for Arvida, my new real estate company, I asked another agent what the interest rates were at the time. He stopped, gave it some thought, shook his head, and said, "I don't know. My customers always pay cash."

Now we're talking!

A month later, in March, Arvida sold an entire condominium building by lottery in one weekend. The building was to be located across the street from the ocean and had not yet broken ground.

Each Arvida agent who had interested parties would draw a number. Agent number one, as determined by drawing numbers, as in a lottery, would call his best customer and ask him which unit he wanted and the buyer would select one he had already decided on. The contract was written, FedExed to him, and expected back by Friday of the next week. The agent then handed over the buyer's deposit check, which he had received earlier. Then Agent number two called his best customer and did likewise.

The sales went so fast the developer complained there wasn't time to raise the prices after the first ten or fifteen sales. In any case the building was sold out, with the buyers giving $30,000 to $40,000 deposits.

The building was completed quickly and by fall it was ready to close. By that time the interest rates had risen to 22 percent for second homes and all the buyers walked away from their deposits rather than close on their units. Their rationale was that they were purchasing the unit to flip to another buyer and it would ultimately cost them less to drop

$30,000 or $40,000 right away than to carry the mortgage indefinitely.

While I was amazed at how casually people seemed to bet such large sums of money, I was shocked at how awful the market had become. Many developers throughout Florida suffered the same fates and were left holding deposits and their empty condominium buildings and/or projects.

Timing is so important in life, and mine, which had always been excellent, suffered a nose bleed. The next two years I eked out a living on $7,000 a year income. If I hadn't been living for free in Mother and Dad's condo, I would never have made it.

As it was, I lived off the developers. Their inventories were so high they went into overdrive in marketing them. Seemingly every week there were one or two open houses at developments. These were not simple little sandwiches-and-cookies affairs. These were major event theme parties with live bands, caterers, prizes, hard liquor, rides, even casino nights, and of course plenty of good food. Some developers gave a Mercedes Benz to the agent selling the most houses in his subdivision. Others gave TV sets, weekends at spas, trips to Hawaii, and so forth.

Incredibly, a woman called the office a couple months after I began working at Arvida. She wanted to see a $900,000 house. I hopped right over there to show it. Trying to think of some way to qualify her, I asked if she and her husband would have to sell a house before purchasing. She gave that some serious thought and replied, "No, I don't think we'll have to sell either one of them." She sounded qualified to me.

But she left town. Said she'd be back in two years! Next year she and her husband would be looking at property on the west coast of Florida, but please send her information on homes between Ft. Lauderdale and Jupiter Beach that were on the Intracoastal Waterway and were under

Boca Raton: A Rarified World

$2 million. What an opportunity. I took it and ran with it.

For the next two years I had my own private house and garden tour of Palm Beach County. Times were tough all over, so when I called agents "up the road" in exclusive Gulfstream or Palm Beach to ask about previewing their listings, they would say, "Well, if they can afford $2 million, they can afford $5 million. Why don't you take a look at these other listings while you're here?" Which, of course, I did.

I learned the difference between "old money" and "new money." Old money had homes decorated in the preppy pinks and greens, dark hunt colors, or perhaps simply faded glory, which is now called shabby chic. Surprising how many were already into "shabby chic." But others were stunning. They had sleek, shiny hard surfaces, soaring ceilings, and lots of glass and open spaces. Very, *very* expensive.

After two years of searching and after finally finding the right house for him, my big customer turned to me and said, "Here is what I think is happening. There are four types of buyers in this market. The first are people with good incomes, but they don't really have a lot of cash in hand, so they are limited in how high they can go. The second are the investors, but their money is tied up in the houses we are looking at, so they are not in the market right now. The third are foreign investors, but the dollar exchange is working against them, so they are out of the market. And then there is the fourth kind, those who simply have a lot of money and have the cash to buy in this price range. That's where I am. So we're going to Australia for six weeks. While I'm gone, I'll have my attorney get in touch with you about the details of the purchase and when I get back, I'll sign the contract."

And that's what he did.

In the course of driving the couple around, we became friendly enough that I eventually asked him how he had made his money, since he had already told me he was a physicist and, in my mind, that wasn't computing into being able to afford multimillion-dollar homes.

His wife replied: "He didn't make his money as a physicist. He has always enjoyed hunting and he turned his hobby into a business selling hunting equipment and outdoor gear. He devised a distribution system for his business, and while it wasn't completely operational, the concept was so good that another company bought his business and hired him back as a consultant."

Not long after that, maybe two or three weeks later, in an interview with Malcolm Forbes, Barbara Walters asked him if there was any way then for a young entrepreneur to create great wealth such as he had done, or were there no such opportunities left. (Obviously, this was before dot-coms were on the horizon!)

Malcolm Forbes leaned back and replied, "Yes, indeed. As a matter of fact, I have a friend who has always enjoyed hunting, and he turned his hobby into a business selling hunting equipment and outdoor gear. He devised a distribution system for his business, and while it wasn't completely operational, the concept was so good that another company bought his business and hired him back as a consultant." Hello.

That one sale took two years.

When I was still the new kid on the block, I needed customers. I thought I'd gotten very lucky when Rachael asked me to hold open her listing of a six-unit waterfront condominium building that started at $500,000. The building was still in its unfinished state with no window sills, no facing on the fireplaces, no floor coverings, nor any trim. There might have been primer on the walls. As we walked through the building, I asked her what the allowances would be since the units were obviously not ready to move into.

She exclaimed in her soft, southern voice, "Loudell, at these prices we don't include allowances. We simply let the buyers finish the units as they choose."

I'm not certain if I had yet made a sale, but I do know I was hungry for a deal. So when a young man went through the building with his girlfriend, I was excited to hear him say how much he liked them. He was an artist and loved the light in the building as well as the views. While this particular building would not accommodate his boat, could I show him some other places? Better believe it; I had nothing else to do.

Then I walked him to his car. It was an old convertible that had obviously escaped from the body shop before the painting had been completed. My heart sank, but I remembered Bill Ahtes's admonition: "Never judge a customer by his dress or by his vehicle. He might be able to buy and sell the whole company, even though he's in his dirty work clothes." Besides, the buyer assured me the car was an antique he was restoring.

We saw many properties and dined at several nice restaurants, usually at his expense, but the time eventually came to put up or shut up; it was time to buy. I'd had it. Either fish or cut bait, but let's get on with it.

The problem was that while I'd shown him townhouses, condos, and houses galore, the light was never right. Forget the style of the house, the room count, or its condition; if the light wasn't right, the property was wrong.

Finally! I found a house with real potential. The light seemed good, the floor plan wasn't bad, the price was just under a half million. Now, if he only had a model with him so he could check out the light better.

"Can I help you?" I asked innocently.

"Well, yes, if you don't mind," he replied in a matter-of-fact voice. "I paint nudes. If you don't mind taking off your clothes, I have a drape in the car trunk I'll run and get."

Without pausing for an answer, he dashed to his car.

Hadn't I recently seen a *60 Minutes* program in which a California Realtor had explained that when her customer had asked *her* to model the hot tub, she had jumped right in? And no, she hadn't had a bathing suit with her at the time. Maybe this is what one did in these high priced areas.

Quick! Make a decision.

One would like to think that I wouldn't have needed much time to ponder this decision, but one would be wrong. Did I mention I was desperate? And I might add that at that time I had a pretty decent figure.

So I went into the powder room of this vacant house and stood there looking in the mirror and saying to myself, *Have you lost your mind?* But I was *in* the bathroom, so that certainly indicated some sort of willingness on my part, didn't it? Now what?

He stood outside, I stood inside. We both waited.

Slowly I took off a scarf, held it outside the door, and dropped it just like a strip teaser. And waited. I couldn't believe I was even doing this much!

Boca Raton: A Rarified World

Well, that was the best I could do. When nothing else followed the scarf, we both realized I wasn't going any further. So we left. He didn't buy the house and I never sold him anything. I *had* discovered something about myself, though: It's a good thing I didn't have a smashing figure or I'd probably have been considering *Playboy*!

In my second year in Florida, the market was still anemic. Customers in Boca were often the owners or top management of businesses or on the boards of large, national corporations. In other words, they had their fingers on the pulse of their businesses and/or the economy, and they were not buying real estate.

One day out of the blue, my manager called me into his office and, without speaking a word, handed me a typed paper. I glanced at it and then slowly read it, barely understanding. I looked up at him and he nodded, yes. It was a thirty-day termination of employment notice.

That was my fourth firing! It was not getting easier. As usual, there was much weeping and wailing. During the course of those thirty days, I turned in a contract of sale for $350,000; the manager said he would rescind the firing. But of course, I'd seen the writing on the wall, so I left.

I ended up around the corner on route A1A at Trade Winds Realty. The difference was like night and day. While I had felt as if I was banging my head against a wall at Arvida, Trade Winds, an all-female company, was friendly, welcoming, and with its location across from the beach, busier. I settled in and thrived.

It seemed to me that every time I've been fired, even though the rejection was awful, it was a beneficial step toward a much better future. There's just no growth without some pain.

The move to Trade Winds marked the beginning of the end of the down market. Over the years the real estate market in Boca Raton came back and my business came back with it. It was a friendly environment among the agents, perhaps because of the hard times we had endured together, along with the socializing that accompanied those times. We had no lockboxes, as we have on houses in Salisbury, so when one showed a house, it was necessary to either pick up the key at the listing agent's office or meet the agent at the house for a showing.

Buyers are rarely faithful in the best of times, and when they have the added protection of anonymity in a place that's not their hometown, they would work with several agents. What they seldom understood was that most agents were competitors, not cut-throats. It wasn't unusual for agents to call one another to report that "Your customer, Mr. and Mrs. Williams, to whom you showed my listing last week, is out with so-and-so today. You'd better touch base with them!"

Once a competitor called to ask if I could arrange for her to show an expensive house located on the Intracoastal Waterway that I had listed the previous year but not sold. The listing was now expired. She had a customer who would be perfect for that house. She could have called the owner directly, but she went through me instead.

As usual I threw myself into my business, in more ways than one. A couple who had relocated to Boca with IBM and had purchased a high-end home from me called to ask if I would find a little condo for them to purchase for their mother. You bet I would.

One of the units I was showing was a golf course-front condo. Since the mother enjoyed walking, I showed them how convenient it would be for her to walk along the edge of the fairway to the club house. Silly me, it was daytime and walking on the cart path might get us killed, so we trudged through the rough. Only it had just been watered, and I was concerned that the water would ruin my new shoes.

Fortunately, there was a practice green nearby, surrounded by an attractive green walkway, so I steered them toward it with the expectation of then heading directly to the clubhouse. There was a slight slope down to the walkway, so as we approached, I took a little hop to reach it.

As I was airborne my customer called out, "Watch out for the water!"

Water? What water?

And with that I landed in the slimy, algae-filled ditch that surrounded the damn practice green. I landed on my hands and knees with my purse floating in the slime. So much for protecting my new shoes.

Undaunted, I stood up, dripping with algae, and pointed to the clubhouse saying, "It would probably be more convenient for her to use the sidewalk over there."

My customer shook her head, laughed a little (she probably laughed hysterically when she told her husband), and declared the showings over for the day. I've often wondered what the people sitting on their balconies must have thought as they watched the dumb blonde Realtor walk over and jump into the ditch. Talk about a bad day!

Buyers stopped by the office with no appointment, expecting to look at property then and there. So it was important to be selective with one's clientele. One didn't want to leave floor duty for a looker when a real buyer was just around the corner, particularly if they were cash buyers in the half-million-dollar range. In Boca I was assigned primary or backup floor duty fourteen or fifteen times a month compared to three or four times in Salisbury.

Often a couple would come in and the man, trying to impress his lady friend or wife, would say he wanted an oceanfront condo. When asked what his price range was, he would say, or imply, there was no limit. "The reason I ask," I would explain, "is because the price ranges from $250,000 to over a million dollars."

"Oh," he would often reply, "let's keep it closer to $250,000."

Over time I learned to quickly size up those walk-ins. There was no time to prequalify them with a lender, so we developed our own methods. What were they driving? What jewelry were they wearing? Matching Rolexes were a good sign; tennis bracelets were too. If they were hot and sweaty from actually playing tennis or working out, even better!

I also learned to value my own time. As harsh as it seems, sometimes one simply had to let some fish swim away. The most extreme example was an Italian American couple who stubbornly asked for an impossible style of oceanfront condo at an equally impossible price and was totally unwilling to compromise. For two days I'd shown them everything I could think of, yet still they demanded more. After yet another frustrating showing, I put them into my car and returned to the office.

"Why are we here?" he asked, puzzled. "When we started out today you said you had three units for us to see, and we've seen only one."

"That's right. But I now realize the other two will not meet your very limiting criteria either, so there is no need for you to see them. It's obvious to me I cannot meet your needs. Perhaps you should try another agent in another area." For a change I was doing the firing.

Once, after working for several days with a young couple, I'd found them a house for $85,000 way west of town. As we sat down to write the contract at 8:00 p.m., they announced that the wife had been taking a real estate course and they wanted to buy the house with FHA financing. Stunned, I stared at her. I had not even been good with this in Salisbury. But here that was a statement one never heard. Finally, I confessed, "You probably know more about this than I do now."

I called my manager, *three lenders at home*, and the listing agent, and none of us could figure out what to do. Finally, I told them that if they had to go FHA, I couldn't help them. And with that, we said good night and went our separate ways.

Another time, as I was leaving with a couple to show oceanfront condos, I asked, as I always do, "Shall we go in my car?"

"No," she replied quite simply, "we'll follow you in the limousine. It's much easier to have the chauffer watch the children while we look at the unit." She was correct, it was a *lot* easier.

Occasionally a customer from Massachusetts would come into my orbit. And without fail I would find some way to bring up the Kennedys. And it seemed without fail they always responded negatively. I began to wonder how Senator Kennedy had ever got elected.

Even though I was living comfortably, I was associating with people who were much wealthier. What I learned with the Kennedys was reinforced once again: even though wealth may separate us, and in some case, it is staggering wealth, we are all still the same under the skin.

In 1986 Jackie Becker and I formed a partnership. Since she went to the Berkshires every summer, she needed someone to cover for her in Boca. Although she socialized in a different stratum from me, she included me at several of her social events. She had a "small" sit-down dinner one evening in her oceanfront condo for about thirty friends. We dined at tables for four scattered throughout the apartment and then gathered later in the living room for the entertainment, which that evening was a magician.

As we chatted, one woman was telling a friend that she and her family had just arrived for spring break and exclaimed over how hectic and frazzled her life had been; with getting the kids home from school and getting them packed, there just wasn't enough time. Didn't she agree that it made things a whole lot simpler to be able to just pile everything onto the plane and then sort it out when you got here? I realized then they used private jets like we used cars. Same concept, different stratum.

Personal computers are so much a part of our lives today, it's difficult to imagine life without them. And of course, once you have a computer at your elbow, there is no giving it up. But I didn't know that when Jackie rushed up to me at work and declared we *must* each get one. She had just returned from the National Association of Realtors convention and had found the ideal software package, Howard and Friends. Little elves in the DOS program were going to help keep track of our business.

Well, who was I to look progress in the eye and say "no thanks" *and* also withstand Jackie's enthusiasm? So even though I had never given a moment's thought to my needing one, I agreed to join her in the computer age. We would be the first in the office to have one.

She took charge and in a couple of days called to say she'd found just what we needed. So after a brief demonstration of how wonderful a computer can be, and with a whole lot of trust, I plunked down my credit card and for $3,000 bought a computer. It would be delivered all loaded and ready to go on Friday. Since I had an appointment then, I told them, "Just put it on my desk and I'll look at it when I get back in." Oh, the innocence of that remark! There it sat when I returned at the end of the day. I was about to begin learning an important lesson.

Boca Raton: A Rarified World

While I may love technology, it doesn't even like me.

I sat in my chair and looked at the blank screen and touched a key, nothing. I looked for an on button but couldn't find one. I asked for help, but since no one in the office had seen a personal computer, there were no suggestions. I looked at the clock and it was 4:45, almost closing time. Quickly I called the store with the first of a lifetime of technical questions.

"How do I turn it on?"

And thus, I entered the computer age. Jackie had found the simplest program imaginable, so once I learned how to start the thing, it was full steam ahead.

Sometimes when I'm struggling with all the different programs everyone has today, I think back to my first simple black-and-white, point-and-click program and long for the good old days.

It was around that time that the office acquired its own fax machine. What a luxury to no longer have to run to a store up the road and pay them to send a fax. Just several months earlier I had been so impressed when a lawyer friend had mentioned that her office had purchased its own fax machine, that with a flush of envy, I had exclaimed over the convenience of having one so handy. She was quick to point out the downside.

"Now, when I tell another attorney toward the end of the day, 'I'll courier the papers to you tomorrow,' they reply, 'No, just fax them to me today.' So I lose the extra hours in the evening I could have had to work on those papers because now they expect the papers by the end of the business day."

Life was speeding up.

Spring Breakers

Although I hit the economic slump when I first arrived, I never had any doubts about being in Florida. I ended up living in my parents' condo for four years, much longer than I had initially planned. Finally, I bought a darling townhouse in Charleston Place in Boca Raton and set up shop.

It wasn't long before spring breakers started arriving. Virginia, my niece, and Marissa Mercado, her college roommate, were the first. I was on the phone with Mother telling her I was ready for them, had a Perdue Oven Stuffer cooked, and food in the house. They hadn't arrived yet but should be there very soon. Mother was concerned about the stories she'd been reading in the paper and hearing on TV about a nightclub called the Button. She was busy emphasizing to me how important it was that I not let the girls go to the Button because people were dancing on the bars and doing obscene things with bananas when the girls bounded into the house saying they really needed to hurry. They'd met some guys on the road and they were all meeting at the Button!

I laughed, hung up with Mother, and said, "Fine. When will you be home?"

Twinkling and giggling they said, "4:00 a.m."

This was a testing-of-the-waters answer, but I really didn't care. So I laid down my only rule: "Don't be late. I'm not staying awake for you so if you are not here when you say you will be, then that's the end of staying with me. My only rule is day or night, be home when you say you will be or call to give me a new ETA."

Spring breaks became a highlight of each year I was there. So much energy. So little effort on my part. I learned quickly not to count on the girls for meals and they learned not to count on me. What could be easier?

Mothers have an awesome instinct about when to check in with their little chickadees. I was reminded of this once again the year Marissa called me at 4:00 a.m. to say they were still in Ft. Lauderdale, too drunk to drive.

"Where are you?" I said, playing the concerned aunt.

"With some guys in their hotel." Or did she say apartment)? "Are you okay?"

"Yes, we're fine, but we aren't going to attempt to drive back tonight."

I was grateful to hear from them on time. "When should I expect you?"

"9:00 a.m."

"Thanks for calling. See you then." I hung up the phone, turned over, and went back to sleep. No questions asked. So much for being the responsible adult.

Now a mother's instincts are more finely honed than a mere aunt's. And I witnessed them in full force the next day. At exactly nine o'clock the girls walked in. We were just sitting down over coffee to rehash the evening's events when the phone rang. It was 9:15 and Jacquie was checking in and checking up on her little chickadee.

I smiled at the girls and smugly said, "They're sitting right here, want to talk to Virginia?" What happened in Boca, stayed in Boca.

Another year everyone seemed to descend at the same time. Virginia and Marissa arrived, of course, plus Virginia's sister, Kristin, and four of her friends who had spring break at the same time. Somehow there would be room for everyone in my two-bedroom home. That year I did have an additional rule: I got to take my shower first before the hot water ran out.

To thank me for being my usual hands-off hostess, the girls planned an evening out for me. The place Virginia had found was called Boggie's in West Palm Beach. It was a strip joint and on Wednesday evenings it was Girls' Night Out.

Of course, we arrived late and all the seats were taken in the main room. However, the bar was adjacent to the room and had a good view, so that became our staging ground. It worked out well, because the girls were so excited that they were popping around here, there, and everywhere—taking pictures, buying drinks, checking things out. It was, "Loudell takes our picture, Loudell do this, Loudell do that."

Finally, the show began and as I stood on my toes to get a better look, the bartender wiped down the bar and offered it as a seat. I accepted. My, but those were good-looking young men in their cute little G-strings, strutting their stuff. There were no victims here as one so often senses when watching women perform stripteases before lecherous men. Here, the rafters were ringing as women screamed and whistled and tucked dollar bills into those well-stuffed G-strings. At the end of the evening so much money had been stuffed into their G-strings, the men looked as if they were wearing tutus! It was great!

The next week Robin, another of Phil and Jacquie's daughters, arrived with her friend. Frustrated that she'd missed all the fun, she insisted that we go to Boggie's on Wednesday. Which we did.

One of the things I missed while living in Boca was that it was too large for people to recognize you when you were shopping or dining out. But that night the bartender at the only strip joint I visited recognized me as we entered, and as he wiped down the counter, he called out in a nice, loud voice, "Hey, Loudell, I've got your seat right here on the bar!" Figures.

One day shortly before I returned to Salisbury, Jackie called and asked if I was busy. No? Then she'd swing by and pick me up for an appointment. In the car she explained that a friend had called to ask her opinion about whether he should put his waterfront home on the market now "as is" or if he should fix it up first and then sell it. He thought the fixing-up part would run about $750,000. What did we think?

The ten-thousand-square-foot waterfront house was in Royal Palm, one of Boca's finest communities. It sat on two lots, so there would be plenty of room for the tennis court. He and his wife showed us around the house, and indeed it looked tired and needed a great deal of "fluffing." He was a banker—well, not just any banker, but the head of a national bank. He had found a new home that he loved in Arizona for eight million dollars. They really hadn't lived in this house for a while, not at all last year, so if he could sell this house and buy a million-dollar oceanfront condo in town (to keep his Florida residence), he could then purchase the other house. What did we think?

We said to fix it up and then sell. As we were leaving, standing at the door, the wife asked Jackie if her son, Richard, was still the pilot for Julio Iglesias. No, he'd suffered an eye injury and couldn't fly commercially anymore; he was now a salesman for Learjets.

"Oh," the wife said, "we've been looking for a plane and had looked at Lear. I'd forgotten how small they are. I think we're going to go with a Gulfstream we saw last week."

This was definitely not my world!

(A couple of years later when I was visiting Boca with Dad, I saw Jackie and asked about the banker. She said they had fixed up the house and fallen in love with it all over again and decided to keep it. However, they did buy the Gulfstream jet and it crashed, killing both of them.)

CHAPTER ELEVEN

A SPIRITUAL JOURNEY

*As long as you derive inner help and
comfort from anything, keep it.*
—Mahatma Gandhi

ne day in the summer of 1988, Mother called. When I answered, she said, "Jacquie says you're going to hell in a handbasket. Is that true?"

"No," I assured her, "I am not going to hell." I knew what she was referring to and wasn't the least bit worried. I had been on a spiritual journey for several years by then and Mother must have been recounting some of my discoveries to Jacquie, who may have found them alarming.

Life was going great guns for me. Business was strong, I loved my house; I had good friends. So why was I waking up in the middle of the night crying out to God, "Help me, help me, please help me, God."

This went on for several weeks. Sometimes I would awaken with tears on my cheeks, always with a prayer on my lips and a plea for help. The answer to my prayers came from an unexpected source.

My journey began when Phil and Jacquie came for a visit. I was unfortunately still in the spring-break entertainment mode; ergo, no food in the house. I walked into the kitchen the first morning in time to overhear Jacquie whispering to Phil, who was about to leave to play golf, "There isn't even a piece of bread in the house!" *Oops!*

That evening after dining out, we walked to a nearby bookstore that had recently opened, and which Jacquie and I had scouted out that afternoon. We knew we were going there for dessert, but we very cleverly disguised our intent by telling Phil we wanted him to see the charming bookstore.

As we strolled around the stacks on our way toward the food, Phil looked up, walked in a straight line to a shelf, took out a book, and handed it to me, saying, "I want to give you this book. It changed my life."

With that kind of endorsement, I could hardly wait to open it. The book, *Heading Toward Omega,* also changed my life. Who would have thought that Phil, of all people, would have hand-delivered God's answer to my prayers? Thus began a spiritual exploration that led me on a slightly divergent path from my traditional religious teachings but was for me a joyous, life-changing journey.

The book was about near-death experiences, which was an entirely new subject to me. I devoured the book and went back to the store, ravenous for more information on life after death. I became a regular customer, haunting the stacks for any spiritual, biblical, motivational, new age, or philosophical books that introduced new avenues of discovery for me. Some were bizarre, others were inspiring, but all were opening my eyes and mind.

There was a woman at the store, perhaps she was a manager, who took me under her wing and would help with my selections by telling me to skip this book, or I wasn't ready for that one, or try this book first before reading that one. Several times I would choose a particular book and she would shake her head and find another one that was more appropriate. It was a strange time, for I simply could not read enough. I was discovering there was an entirely different way to know God and it was okay.

Since I have never been someone to stay within the lines, I enjoyed the freedom to escape the box of traditional religion in order to check out different approaches and ideas. A friend/client called one day and asked if I would be interested in attending a Shirley MacLaine seminar in Orlando with her. She was to teach meditation. Yes, yes, I would love to go.

For two days Shirley MacLaine spoke without notes on New Age topics that were so far over my head I had no idea what she meant. But she also conducted three meditations that were fantastic. She showed us what and where our chakras are and how to relax and quiet our minds so our higher selves could be heard. She spoke of past-life experiences, of controlling our bodies with thought, and of the enormous power of thought/prayer when it is united with those of others and directed to a particular goal. I was enthralled.

I returned home and read even more voraciously. One particular book transformed me. When I went to check out the book, my little manager/guide shook her head and said it was too difficult and it was probably too soon for me to try reading it, just as she had done several other times. But this time I was determined. Declaring I felt I was ready, I purchased it and headed for home

Well, *A Course in Miracles* was the most difficult book I've ever read. The best I could do was read a paragraph at a time, go back, highlight certain passages, and then reread the entire paragraph before finally moving on to the next paragraph. I began waking each morning at six o'clock to reread all the highlighted sections I had read the previous day. That night I would begin the next chapter. Thus, I was able to read the thirty-one chapters in a little over a month.

In addition, there was a 365-day student's manual with daily lessons that I read and followed faithfully for the entire year. I became a new person. What I came to accept is that Truth is constant. It cannot change. If it changes, it was not Truth. If God is absolute love and loves mankind as Jesus taught, then He cannot change, regardless of what we do, individually or collectively. Love gives all and requires nothing. It is like the sun; after millennia of shining on the earth, the sun doesn't suddenly say, "Earth, you owe me." The sunshine is constant even if sometimes it is too intense and we turn our backs on it, or put barriers between it and us. It doesn't stop shining because of our choices; it's still there when we awaken in the morning.

And just so, God's love is perpetual. It is there for each one of us, whatever we do. We may turn away from it, we may say we don't need or want it, but when we look for it, it is there waiting. Therefore, I realized that God has no needs. We may create a story, or a scenario, or a reason why we must do something, anything to deserve His love; we can even believe that if we aren't careful, we could lose it and make Him angry. But in the end, just like the sun, His love still shines on us; we have only to accept it.

I had immersed myself in all kinds of spiritual readings and eventually found at the end of the process that the faith I had had when I was younger, in South America, had been enhanced, enlarged, and definitely strengthened.

So, when Mother called, I assured her I would be fine.

A Spiritual Journey

It was an incredible time then. It seemed that almost everyone I touched had a supernatural experience to tell me about. Judi, one of Trade Winds' partners, told me of a friend who had died, and when Judi returned home from the funeral, there, mysteriously, on Judi's pillow was a camellia, her friend's favorite flower.

Another friend recounted having a vision of her father at the moment of his death. At the time, she was driving along A1A in Florida and her father was at home in another state.

Another had an astral projection in which she traveled to California and saw her relatives as they sat in their home knitting and watching TV. Later she confirmed with them that they had been doing exactly that at the time she was "there."

Perhaps you have heard or read something about bringing into your life that which you think about or dwell on. In those days, there was no such discussion, but I was certainly experiencing it, because many people, sometimes even strangers, would tell me about their own supernatural encounters.

In 1989 there was a buzz about a book on the experiences of Dr. Brian Weiss, chief of psychiatry at a large, university-affiliated hospital in Miami, who hypnotized a patient who then regressed to a past life. Dr. Weiss's book was fascinating. A customer had told me Dr. Weiss was speaking at a synagogue in Ft. Lauderdale, so I bought two tickets and met Virginia at my door upon her arrival for some R&R.

"Quick," I demanded, "you have to decide right now if you want to come with me to hear this man talk about past-life experiences. If you don't want to come, fine, stay here, but I'm going!" Virginia dropped her stuff and jumped in the car.

Well, it was an eye-opener for her. There were people wandering everywhere with crystals hanging around their necks; there were crystals for sale, and people talking about their chakras and psychic experiences. Dr. Weiss opened his talk with a simple statement, "I'm here to tell you that you don't die. That's my entire message."

Then he looked up at the audience and continued. "How I arrived at this conclusion is my story." And then he told us an incredible tale of a patient who had had over eighty life experiences, which he had recorded while she was under hypnosis. By the end of the evening, Virginia was wearing a crystal.

Later I was telling yet another customer about the book and she said, yes, she had not only read his book, but at some point, before the book was published and while attending a psychiatric seminar (the subject under discussion being hypnosis), she had met the author's wife. As they were washing their hands in the ladies' room, Mrs. Weiss exclaimed, "You should hear what my husband is hearing from a patient he's hypnotizing. She's regressing into many past lives."

Interestingly enough, the last chapter of *Many Lives, Many Masters* refers to a psychic in South Miami Beach to whom the patient ended up going for another verification of her past lives. The psychic was the same one my friends and I had gone to on several occasions and found to be very accurate.

Meditation became important to me. And sometimes as I meditated, I would have insights. They were simple, basic such as this one, but reassuring. They helped to make me conscious of life's bigger pictures.

Life with its troubles and pressures is like being in a small boat in rough waters—alone—trying to reach a safe harbor. As you struggle first with the sails and then the tiller, with the water splashing over the sides threatening to swamp the boat, it's very frightening.

However, reaching the entrance to a safe harbor is not enough. To actually reach safety, one must navigate very carefully, for there are still numerous dangers along the way. It is terrifying to feel so insignificant, so helpless.

Then God says, "Trust Me. I will see you safely to shore. Let go of the tiller; do not try to steer your boat or adjust the sails. You need do nothing. Trust Me."

There is the rub. With so much danger around you, so many opportunities to make a mistake and drown, can you let go? Can you trust God enough to not grab the tiller when the boat is lurching toward the rocks?

Can you trust God when the sails are flapping out of control—or maybe when the boat suddenly becomes becalmed? As the little boat shifts course and heads in a strange direction, one you are confident can't be right, will you take control again or trust God?

God will bring us safely to shore—if we trust Him. It's the trusting that's so difficult. Too many times we reach for the tiller—we want to be in charge—when, if we had trusted Him, He would have brought us through the danger.

Sometimes doing nothing is *the best way; if we are listening to God.*

Saying Good-Bye

Time was marching on and with it came a sense that my time in Florida was winding down. The past several springs, as my parents prepared to return to Salisbury, I would watch Mother and wonder if she would be returning the next fall. But each summer Phil would fix her up, and she and Dad would come back to Florida. Perhaps there is a special angel who watches over senior citizens there, for certainly Mother and Dad were protected.

They returned home in April of 1989. By June Mother was in the hospital with chest pains. Dad had driven her there, dropped her off, and let her check herself in. He needed to drive home before it was too dark. There was an Orioles' night game that probably weighed heavy on his mind too.

In any case, she sounded good whenever I spoke to her on the phone that week and although her tests were okay and she was ready to check out, Phil had arranged for her to stay another day or so as a precaution. Good thing he did because that Saturday night Dad called to say with tears in his voice, "Your mother has taken a turn for the worse and I don't think she's going to be leaving the hospital. You had better come home."

Dad's ominous call had come in the late evening on Saturday, July 1. Just as I had done in 1971 when she had had her first heart attack and Phil and Dad had reached me at our little McLean hideaway, I began packing and preparing to leave for an indefinite period. Just as before, I sort of watched myself from afar as I calmly made my plans and the next morning made my way to Salisbury and an uncertain future.

Phil explained during the drive from the Salisbury airport to the hospital that Mother was in cardiac failure and that there didn't seem to be anything to do to help her, barely anything to ease her discomfort. No one thought she could overcome this, her latest medical battle. When I arrived, I saw immediately that, unlike the last time, this time there would not be a happy ending.

She turned to me when I walked into her room, smiled weakly, and said she was glad to see me. What could I say to her? "Hi, thought I'd drop in to see how you are doing. Just happened to be in the area." We both knew she was dying. There really wasn't anything to say, except I love you.

As I sat at her bedside watching her and sometimes sharing a smile with her, we communicated silently all the love we had for each other. She had very expressive eyes and when she would awaken from a nap, she'd look at me, smile a little, and seem to say, "You're still here? I knew you would be. I love you."

She was a lady. Except for "shit," which was her favorite word, I don't think I ever heard her utter another foul word. She was gracious to everyone, but she had strong opinions on many things, and you always knew how she felt if you were on the wrong side of that opinion.

In the 1960s, when segregation was still the order of the day, Mother did her volunteer work at the Junior Board Shop in our community hospital. One day a nicely dressed older black couple came into the shop for lunch. And although there were seats available at the counter, Mother had to tell them they would have to take their lunch outside. They didn't make a fuss, but Mother did. By the time she reached home, she was fuming. She declared to Dad, to me, and to anyone else in hearing distance, "That is the last time I'm doing that. Those were very nice people and I was embarrassed to tell them to eat outside. The next time I'm working at the shop, I'm not turning anyone away. If people don't like it, they can go outside."

She was my drinking buddy. Actually, she was mine and Jacquie's drinking buddy. And it was Mother who, after hearing some of the tales of Phil's infamous fortieth birthday, turned to both of us and asked in the driest of voices, "Can we burn that recipe now?"

She died at two o'clock in the morning on the Fourth of July. She had been a wonderful person. So gentle—so feisty. She had been the sunshine of our lives, the optimist who overcame Dad's worry. The organizer. She was the one who always encouraged me to color outside the lines, to push the envelope, to dare to be different. Mother gave me courage.

We canceled her bridge game for Tuesday and scheduled her funeral for Friday. On Saturday I asked Dad if he needed me to come home to live with him and he said yes.

CHAPTER TWELVE

WHO SAYS YOU CAN'T GO HOME AGAIN?

> *I see friends shaking hands, saying "How do you do?" They're really saying, "I love you."*
> *And I say to myself, what a wonderful world.*
> "What a Wonderful World"
> —Louis Armstrong

It took longer this time to pack up and move back to Maryland than it had when I moved to Florida ten years earlier. To begin with, I had recently begun managing Trade Winds Realty's new branch office and leaving would put them into some tough straits. We had not even had our official opening of the office, so I promised to stay for that, which looked like it would be after Thanksgiving.

And of course, I had to sell my townhouse, and the market was turning south. I don't know why I always buy high and sell low, but that seems to be my trend. Meanwhile I told Dad to start looking for a house with my friend Bernie, since the condo would be too small for us. I figured it would occupy him for a while. The next day he wrote an offer. *Damn.* I never get customers who work that fast!

Dad moved into the house on Crestview Lane in November. I moved in on December 15 in the snow. Two days earlier I had been walking around barefoot in Boca, saying my farewells. Then I had headed north. And the day after that, I hit an ice storm. As I dressed in my motel, I could hear my neighbors go outdoors and begin making noises around their car. As I strapped on my sandals, it dawned on me they were scraping ice off their windshield! I had no scraper—I didn't even have closed-toe shoes!

North Carolina had had an ice storm the previous night. Only one lane was open on I-95 and it ran at the snail's pace of twenty-five miles an hour. The good news was that the sky was crystal blue, the sun sparkled on the icy trees, making them look almost ethereal, and I had my New Age music. I was content.

It had taken all day to reach home from North Carolina and when I arrived, Dad was in a frenzy of worry about me. Phil, who had been keeping Dad company, bolted for home, having endured all he could of holding his hand. Dad was dissolving into tears of misery, deep into a pity party for himself and, frankly, I didn't blame him. The house was only partially furnished while it awaited my stuff, and it looked very unappealing. Welcome home.

The house was darling, and with my stuff filling in the numerous holes and the household coming into a normal mode, Dad became less lost and more optimistic, so life became better and he stopped crying.

There was quite an adjustment for me, too. For most of the past eighteen years, I had lived alone, coming and going as I wished. Now there were two or three daily meals to prepare, someone wanting an accounting of where I'd been, when I'd return. Someone who at times was simply a friend but at other times unexpectedly returned to parental mode. So together we adjusted: Dad to being single, I to being... not so single.

As Dad stopped weeping, he began looking around. One day, his eyes aglow, he described a woman he'd met at the Ward Museum. Nothing would do but that he should call her for a date. With much discussion of the pros and cons, we decided lunch on Wednesday would be best. He couldn't read the phone book, so I helped him with the number and he was off and running.

Lunch was a success; now he needed something else. Oh, joy, Virginia was having a cocktail party and we could both bring dates. In fact, it was that very weekend. Back to the phone. Were my ears deceiving me or did Dad's voice just become husky and sexy? From the tone of his voice, he was obviously shmoozing a woman. Apparently, it's true; some things you don't forget how to do.

I may not have had children, but I was beginning to see how it is when the kid's hormones kick in! I double dated with my *father*. I drove with my date up front and Dad and his date in the backseat.

At the end of the evening, he walked her to the door while we waited in the car. He seemed very pleased with himself on the way home.

The next morning over breakfast I gave him a little advice. "Cool it a bit. Don't rush things too much."

The words were still hanging in the air when the phone rang. With his eyes dancing, Dad looked at me as he spoke in that deep, husky voice I was beginning to recognize.

"Oh, you liked it? All night, really? Well, I'm delighted you enjoyed it; I thought you might."

I could hardly wait for him to hang up. "What was that all about?"

"That was Peggy," he said with a cat's-eaten-the-canary smile all over his face, "calling to say she liked the book I gave her."

"What book?"

"The one I gave her when I walked her to the door last night. You know, *The Bridges of Madison County*. She thinks I'm very sensitive."

So did all the other women he gave it to! Good ole Mr. Sensitivity.

At a cocktail party Phil and Jacquie gave not long after my return, I found myself alone on the porch with Dave, a local attorney. Both of us were standing looking at the view when he said to me, "You think you can come back here and pick up where you left off, don't you? Well, you can't. Those people who were your friends or your customers won't trust you anymore. They'll think you'll leave again. You're never going to have their confidence again. So you may as well leave now."

After the shock of what he said wore off, instead of reacting indignantly as I wanted to, I tried to evaluate what he had said. Deciding that his comments had some merit and offered a valuable insight, I made it a point to work into my conversations that I was back for good.

One of the wonderful things about returning to Salisbury was the opportunity to be involved in community activities. How I had missed that in Boca. There I had learned a hard lesson, that willingness to be involved in a community does not always translate into finding the right doors open. Here people called to ask me to join their organizations—it was as if I were fresh meat that the carnivores were sniffing it out. My biggest problem was learning to say, "No!"

Friends of Coastal Hospice asked me to become an incoming president, working my way upward to the role over the next four years. The chamber of commerce asked me once again to be a member of the board of directors. Eventually I also became chair of the Beautification Committee, which I have held for over thirteen years, helping to make Salisbury a more beautiful place to live. I served briefly on other boards and when Dad resigned from the John B. Parsons Foundation, they asked me to replace him.

Since then, I've served on the boards of Habitat for Humanity in Wicomico County, the city park advisory committee, Urban Salisbury's sculpture committee, and been a participant in many other civic, church, and professional affairs. And most of all, my efforts to raise money to provide goats for desperate families around the world through the Heifer Organization has brought me enormous pleasure as I watch how just one person can make a difference.

I know where my strong instincts for community service come from. Mother had led the junior board at the hospital and both parents were active in our church. Dad had also been president of Rotary, as had Phil. Both father and son had been leaders in the hospital. And perhaps it also comes from my exposure to the Kennedys and the depth of their belief in public service. Robert Kennedy spoke eloquently of the great impact one has when one reaches out to help others, even if it's in the smallest of ways. He summed it up eloquently in his Day of Affirmation Address at the University of Capetown, South Africa in 1966:

> *"It is from numberless diverse acts of courage and belief that human history is shaped. Every time a [person] stands up for an ideal or acts to improve the lot of others or strikes out against injustice, he sends forth a tiny ripple of hope; and crossing each other from a million different centers of energy and daring, those ripples build a current which can sweep down the mightiest walls*

of oppression and resistance."

Being involved in my community has enriched my life. And through that involvement, I have learned what others have discovered before me, that—as Brian Buffini, my real estate business coach, often says—"What you give out in slices is returned to you in loaves."

Again, it was February before I got my license straightened out and Mark Holloway, now my manager, found a desk for me in the designated smoking section of the office. But I was back for good.

Irony is a bittersweet pill. My first listing after returning was $85,000. The world had definitely turned once again. (With amusement I would remember that when Mother and Dad decided to sell their condo in Florida for $75,000, I had referred it to a local agent and told them I wouldn't take a referral fee for it; I was too embarrassed at how low the listing price was.) To make matters more alarming, when I told my seller the termite inspection cost to her could run between forty-five and sixty dollars, she stopped me and said, "Which will it be? Forty-five dollars? Or sixty dollars?" I shuddered to think that fifteen dollars was going to make or break this listing! I definitely wasn't in Boca anymore.

So God must have had a smirk on His face when I took a listing for $18,000. It sat there for quite a while, until Christmas Day as a matter of fact. Someone called about the house, and since I was sitting at home with not much to do except wait for Jacquie to put on another of her wonderful Christmas dinners, I jumped at the chance to show the house.

He liked it. He wrote an offer of $15,000 with owner financing. I reached the seller in Florida, and he countered at $11,500. I paused and stated the obvious: "You're going in the wrong direction."

He said, "I'll go less if I don't have to hold financing." And so on Christmas Day I sold a *house* for $11,500. And God got me for working on Christmas because I never had so many problems with a house as I did with that one. When it finally closed, I probably broke even; certainly, I didn't make a profit with all the time and FedExing involved.

It didn't matter. Now I understand that for me the joy of working in real estate comes with helping clients realize their goals. There is a puzzle involved in most transactions. Matching the buyers with the best possible house that fits their needs and budget is thrilling. And as the sellers' agent, I simply love to market houses and get the best price.

Sometimes I'll think about what I might do if I were not in real estate. But then I realize I am doing exactly what I love to do, whether it's selling a house for peanuts or for millions.

Loudell and Joanna Abercrombie's postcard announcing her transition into retirement while I continue on

The Lion of the Senate

Congress passed the lead paint law—or, as they called it, the Residential Lead-Based Paint Hazard Reduction Act of 1992—and this time I felt the impact of Senator Kennedy's perseverance. When I worked for him in the '60s one of his pet issues was his concern for children living in tenements who, because the landlord was not maintaining the building properly, ingested lead paint from chipping and peeling paint. Lead poisoning causes mental retardation and in severe cases death. When I am explaining this law to customers, I visualize my hand reaching into the file drawer for the senator's lead-paint speech as he prepared to give it one more time. It took him almost twenty-five years, but eventually he got the legislation passed—a fine example of perseverance, of being willing to eat an elephant (no pun intended) one bite at a time. It's good legislation but now I'm stuck with living with the regulations!

At some point my friend Loretta persuaded me to go back to the hill for the senator's annual Christmas party. The staff eggnog party had morphed into a huge Christmas open house in the Senate Caucus Room. It was open to everyone, and the room was filled with Democratic and Republican staffers and some elected officials from all over the hill. As was his custom, the senator and his then-fiancée, Vicki, were dressed in full costume. That year it was Beauty and the Beast. Of course, there was singing, as there always was at his parties. People wonder why he was such a successful senator; well, here is an example of building bridges with people on both sides of the aisle.

I had a friend, Neilie Casey, who died in the terrorist attack on the twin towers in New York City. Senator John Kerry attended her memorial service in Massachusetts, but not Senator Kennedy, who was probably at another person's service. Sensing my disappointment that he had not been there for my friend's service, her mother called me a week or so later.

"I want you to hear this," she proudly said as she pushed the button on her answering system to play back a recording.

And there was Senator Kennedy's voice assuring Anne that even though he had missed connecting with her at least five times, he was not giving up until they talked. Over the years, on the anniversary of that awful day, he touched base with her and the other survivors. And when vandals stole a brass plate from her daughter's memorial, it was Senator Kennedy who generated enough publicity to force the perpetrators to fork over the plaque. He was always taking care of his constituents and nibbling away at issues. That's how he succeeded when Republicans in his home state would have voted him out in a heartbeat. And that's why they celebrated his life. Not only was he a good, caring person, but he also had become an outstanding legislator.

The Senator died of brain cancer on Tuesday, August 25, 2009. His funeral was to be on Saturday, August 29th. My friends urged me to join them in Washington for his funeral, which I longed to do. But that Saturday I was entertaining fifty clients and friends at my home and could not do so. All day I kept an eye on the TV watching the progress of his body being taken from Massachusetts to Washington to Arlington Cemetery.

At one point I was in the kitchen getting something for a guest when I heard the commentor say, 'Joseph and Rose Kennedy had four sons who died. Three of them died violent deaths. Ted Kennedy was the only brother to die in his own bed." He was 77.

A Legacy of Love

Living with Dad for thirteen years was a joy because I was able to know him while I was an adult. Without everyone's help, there would have been times I would have pulled my hair out, but mostly I had learned how to tolerate the times he reverted to the parent role and tossed out the guilt parents always seem to feed their children.

Sometimes I felt as if I were a fish swimming in a stream, watching as Dad cast about with that "parental" bait. I usually refused to rise to it. And because I didn't take the bait too often, we learned to have a congenial life together. And because of Phil and Jacquie's support, and Virginia popping in with her kids, there was always someone to watch over Dad.

In the fall of 2001 Jacquie and I were comparing calendars. It was terribly frustrating to discover we had both scheduled ourselves to be out of town at the same time in February. She and Phil were going to the islands with their friends the Reddishes; I had plans to attend a business meeting in Miami, for which I had already purchased the tickets. Jacquie said they couldn't cancel their plans, and I didn't want to cancel mine. Their nonrefundable deposit had been paid. They would be gone for two weeks. I would be gone for less than a week.

Jacquie encouraged me get a sitter for Dad and to not give up my trip. Since I really wanted to go to Miami, I said I'd think about it. After all, Dad had been feeling well lately, although I could see he was getting tired of life. More and more often I would think to myself, "He's ready to go if he can only figure out how to do it." He didn't like to be left alone, and he definitely didn't like sitters. I didn't know what to do.

As the time approached to make a final decision, the more torn I became until finally I burst into tears while driving the car one December day and began arguing with God. Pounding my fist on the steering wheel as I drove, going nowhere but heading north, I shouted at God through my tears:

"You said You would always be there for me! That all I had to do was ask and You would answer. Knock and You would open the door. Trust You and You would guide me. Well, I need help! I don't know what to do!"

This one-way conversation went on for a number of miles, and then suddenly an incredible peace descended upon me. Like the snap of your fingers, my tears disappeared. I turned the car around and headed for home with a quiet certainty in my heart. I never gave another thought to my trip—I had my answer. Stay home.

Because Dad's mother had had a stroke and had been completely bedridden for the last three years of her life, he was always concerned about a slow, lingering death. He used to say he wasn't afraid of death; it was the dying he didn't look forward to.

However, the first week of Phil and Jacquie's vacation, Dad turned to me and said, "You know, I think I'm going to die very suddenly and from something strange."

I pooh-poohed it as many grown children will do when their parents are discussing their deaths.

On Saturday afternoon of that week, Dad complained so strongly about his hernia and how painful it was that I called Dave, a former partner of Phil's who lived around the corner. Dad arranged to see him on Monday at Dave's office. But if the pain returned, we were to call and Dave would come to the house to see him. Sunday morning at seven o'clock we called.

When he arrived and examined Dad, Dave said he could repair the hernia and there was an operating room available right then if he wanted to do it. They discussed the pros and cons of it, one doctor to another, and decided to take the chance.

On the way to the hospital, Dad turned to me and exclaimed in a somewhat excited tone of voice, "Remember what I said last week? That I would die from something strange? This is strange."

Once again, I pooh-poohed the thought. But I had already been remembering that earlier comment.

Dad was actually excited. In the pre-op room where the nurse and anesthesiologist were trying to take his history, Dad regaled them with stories of his early days of practice. Finally, I said, "Dad, you have to stop talking. The doctor needs to take your history."

He laughed and replied, "Well, just let me finish this one last story."

When he finished, he looked at me and said, "Don't tell Phil about this; he'll just worry, and there's no need for him to come home early." I assured him I wouldn't.

But he bled, and they needed to operate again that evening. Even before we could finally call to tell Phil what was happening, he and Jacquie were on the phone checking in.

By Tuesday, February 12, Dad was up and walking to the nurses' station. Virginia and I had played hospital tag all day—first she would be there, then I, and then she. But each time I was there, one of his doctors stopped by and said how well he was doing.

Phil called at five o'clock that evening, and he and Dad laughed and joked and had a wonderful visit. I went home for some dinner, and an hour later, while Virginia and I were complimenting ourselves over the phone about how well we were covering the hospital, a call beeped in. It was Dave. Dad had collapsed just as the nurse was removing his dinner tray. He didn't think he would make it.

When Virginia and I arrived, he was indeed dead. Both Dad and I had had our prayers answered. How enormously grateful I was that I was there and not in Miami, where I would have been if God had not answered my prayer in December. And Dad's prayer was answered. He had not lingered even a moment but instead had had an easy death.

God welcomed home his good and faithful son. Dad's faith had been the rock-solid center of his life. I don't recall a time while I was growing up that Dad failed to say his evening prayers on his knees before going to bed. In times of crisis, he had always been the one we leaned on and came to for reassurance and guidance.

Our parents left Phil and me a very precious legacy. There was never any doubt in either of our minds that we were loved equally by our parents. There were no favorites. And because of that, there were no festering issues left unresolved at either departing. How fortunate Phil and I had been to have two such loving, generous parents.

EPILOGUE

Where had I found the courage to be my own person? Independence is lovely, but it can also be lonely with no one to push you, encourage you, or help you reach further. On the other hand, there is no one pulling you back, discouraging you, limiting you, and changing you. But I was never really alone. I was surrounded by love.

As I look back, I see the small choices along the way that led to the decisions that sent me one way or another. Now I can see God's hand at work as I turned toward the more challenging paths. It is in looking back at my life that I realize there are no coincidences and nothing happens by chance. I brought into my life that which I needed or wanted. At the time it was happening, I thought I was making decisions based on happenstance and whim. With hindsight I realize that just as the body craves certain foods—like green vegetables or fruits—to balance and sustain itself, my soul craved certain experiences and circumstances; hence, what I describe as "God's hand on my shoulder" was my soul saying, "Enough of this; time for some of that."

The Kennedy years, the firings, Outward Bound, the Florida years—all these and more strengthened me, prepared me, and helped me to enjoy, tolerate, persevere, and trust. I became a better person. Life is what we make it—and then it is how we regard it; whether life has been good, bad, or nothing much really depends on our perceptions.

As Charles Swindoll says, "When my attitudes are right, there is no barrier too high, no valley too deep, no dream too extreme, no challenge too great for me."

What an incredibly positive experience Outward Bound had been for me. I came away feeling there was not one thing in the world I could not do if I had the right coach. Outward Bound has had a profound influence on my life. My willingness to risk leaving a successful real estate career in Salisbury and move to Florida, where I knew no one, and to reinvent myself there, came from the confidence I had gleaned from Outward Bound.

It certainly prepared me for the hard times that were ahead. When I was suffering my first year in Florida, eking out a paltry living, my former manager called to say there was still a place for me there if I wanted to return. It meant so much to have his vote of confidence, but at the same time, I knew I had it in me to persevere until the good times returned, so I remained in Florida. And because I remained and endured, I became a stronger individual, as well as a better Realtor. When I eventually returned to Salisbury, I felt as if I'd had a master's course in real estate. I had been enriched not just by the people I'd met, but by the selling experiences I'd had as well.

And because I'd had the courage to remain in Florida, I was in the right place when I was ready to begin my spiritual journey.

There are many who believe there are no coincidences in life. That what manifests in one's life is what we bring into it by the choices we make, the questions we ask, and the beliefs we adhere to. My incredible spiritual growth had occurred because in Boca I met a number of remarkable people who helped me to find my way. If they had been in Salisbury, I doubt I would have found them. In fact, I know I have had the hand of God on my shoulder guiding me. He has been there always; the difference is now I recognize it.

And because of my spiritual growth, I was able to enjoy, not just endure, living with Dad. In turn, he enriched my life in many ways.

Over the years I have discovered that life is a gift to be lived day by day. In fact, we even describe "now" as the "present." Each choice we make in life takes us down this path or that path. Some are so well trodden they are easily traversed. Others are less well traveled, and that is where we are shaped, and grow and become who we are. It is the unexpected twists and turns, the detours and obstacles on the bumpy roads of life that we remember, often with fondness. While on the superhighways of life, where we can easily speed along without a challenge, without a thought, we are oblivious to the wonders around us.

I've been blessed in this life to have taken many of the less traveled paths.

And as Robert Frost so poetically stated, "That has made all the difference."

ACKNOWLEDGMENTS

Encouragement to reach for something you never dreamed of doing comes in many forms. First and foremost is my niece, Virginia Brennan, who encouraged me by laughing at my stories as I wrote each one of them. Her laughter or her curiosity about events that happened when she was just a child encouraged me to write more. Without her enjoyment of my stories, I never would have taken it to the next step: printing them.

Janice Nichols edited my first efforts, and she encouraged me by being the first "outsider" to say she enjoyed it. She cleaned up so many grammatical errors, had me clarify other parts, that the first effort was surely improved by her gentle touch.

For those of you reading this book, I should explain here that I originally published a version of it for my family and friends. When Bob Bahr of Factor Press asked me how many copies I wanted to print, I replied, "Let me jot down who would actually want to read it." I came up with fifty names. That was obviously too small a number for the expense, so I printed two hundred copies, which I shared with family and friends. I was overwhelmed by their responses as they passed their books to others.

One of the friends I gave my book to was Paul Strickland, a high school classmate now living in California. He's a Republican, but he's still a very nice person. Paul is a four-term elected school board trustee in Valencia who is running for the Thirty-Eighth California Assembly District in 2012. When he said he enjoyed it and that with some reorganization and additional Kennedy stories, I could actually sell the book, I was thrilled. With his help and encouragement, I did rework most of the book.

Then my cousin Carter Campbell stepped in when I was having second thoughts. His encouragement to think even bigger kept my focus on the ball.

And finally, my friends who continued to ask for the book long after I had run out gave me that final push to actually move forward with this new, fuller book. If you have enjoyed my efforts, then perhaps there is someone in your life you could encourage to reach beyond her dreams and actually try to live them.

www.ingramcontent.com/pod-product-compliance
Lightning Source LLC
LaVergne TN
LVHW040137080526
838202LV00042B/2936